Wind in the Pines

By Curt Iles

*"In the pines, in the pines,
Where the sun never shines,
And you shiver when the cold wind blows"*

- Old mountain folk song

Copyright 2004 by Curt Iles. All rights reserved.
No part of this book may be reproduced, in any manner, without written permission from the author.

ISBN 0 – 9705236- 1 - 0

Unless otherwise noted all scriptures are taken from the Holy Bible, New International Version, Copyright 1973, 1978, 1984 by the International Bible Society. Used by permission of Zondervan Publishing House. Scriptures marked "KJV" are from the King James Version.

CONTACT INFORMATION
Creekbank Publishing
P.O. Box 332
Dry Creek, Louisiana 70637
curtiles@aol.com
www.creekbank.net

Other titles by the author:
Stories from the Creekbank
The Old House

Printed by: Wise Publications
809 East Napoleon
Sulphur, Louisiana 70663
(337) 527-8308

Front cover: Terry Iles sits with his faithful friend, Ivory. This picture was taken in the pines near the Iles family homestead, affectionately known as "The Old House." Cover design by Jason Foux.

Dedication

To my sweet wife of twenty-five years, DeDe - My best friend and life partner. There is no way I could do anything I do without you beside me. Thanks for always believing in me.

Acknowledgements

So many folks, too numerous to name, have encouraged me in writing. I especially appreciate our camp staff who have stood by me through the years. Many friends have helped, especially James Newsom, Kevin and Cathy Willis. Editing assistance has been provided by Terry Iles, Laura Boggs, Courtney Glaser, and Colleen Iles Glaser. I especially appreciate Larry Wise of Wise Publications for his helpful editorial assistance in putting this book together.

Preface-

You Can't Stand by the Same River Twice

This third book, *Wind in the Pines*, is different from my previous books. Here is how I know - because I am different. The native Indians had a saying, "You can't stand by the same river twice." By this statement they meant several things:

First of all, when you return to a river after a period of time, it will have changed. The steady flow of the current, mixed with floodwaters and the hammer of erosion will cause a river to both look and be different from your last visit.

Several times each year I go on canoe trips down the Ouiska Chitto River. I'm always amazed after nearly a year how the river has a completely different look.

Recently I was on the river and came to a place commonly called 'the whirl hole.' It is the deepest place on the river. It gets its name from the fact that the river is coming out of a sharp bend and the water swirls in a whirlpool at this deep spot. Many times I've seen swimmers dive into the deep area of the river and still not be able touch the bottom.

The whirl hole has always been a scary place to me. I've known of several young men who have drowned there. So on our canoe trips from the camp, we usually bypass stopping here.

For years on the east bank there was a high cliff bordered by a steep sand bar. The opposite bank was wooded and had very little open sand.

On this past summer's canoe trip the whirl hole had taken on a completely new personality. The high cliff and sand bar on the near bank had washed away and a large sand bar is now building up across the creek.

Old fallen trees and obstacles are gone, and newly fallen trees lay across what was open water last year. Yes, the river changes, day by day, year by year.

You can't stand by the same river twice... But I think there is a deeper meaning of this saying. I realize why you can't stand by the same river twice...

because when you return, <u>you</u> are no longer the same... just like the river...

... Yes, rising and falling, gaining and losing, growing and dying... we are always changing - all at the same time...

So *Winds in the Pines* is not an attempt to recreate either of my previous books. It is a fresh collection of stories from my heart... written from the place I am currently at as I stand beside the river.

Since we last visited, many changes have occurred in my life:

Two of my sons have left home and are recently married. Although my boys now appear less frequently in my writing, I am still as proud of Clay, Clint, and Terry as ever.

Just like each of you, I've endured hardships and challenges that are a part of life. I've lost loved ones and seen new birth... I have lost one of the major influences of my life...my Dad. I hope my stories about him shed light on what a wonderful man and father he was. I've also experienced the tragic death of a lifelong special friend, Ricky Gallien. I hope the bright light of Ricky's life shows through in the stories where he is mentioned.

I've seen so many good things happen.- I've made life changing trips to Central America, China, Cambodia, and Vietnam. I've seen how other parts of the world live… and it is much different than our way of life. It has filled me with great gratitude for the freedom and blessings I have as an American.

I'm now several miles down the road from a bout of depression in 2000 that laid me low… Hopefully the brokenness, joy, and healing I've experienced come through transparently in my writing.

I've been privileged to be part of a ministry where God is working and I get to witness thousands of lives changed by His power. My wish is that the love of God shines through in these stories about the work of Dry Creek Camp.

Most of all, I've grown… I believe I'm a better man than when those first two books were written. As a reader, I hope you sense that I've been stretched and made more "usable."

I still have something fresh to say, share, and write. Because of that, my heart still has a passion to write and share. Not because I'm an expert on anything - but simply because there is so much to share about the beauty of life.

Finally, I continue to write because of the "ripple effect of writing." When our words are put on paper and make their way into a book, those words will travel to people and places we could never go. I'll have the opportunity to "meet" and affect folks, like you, that I may never know face to face. People have been asking when this next book was going to be out. Well, here it is. Somehow it has found its way into your hands. I hope it now finds its way into your heart.

Because that's what I am… a writer of the heart. The heart is where my stories spring from, and if you are affected by my writing (and I hope you will be!) it will be by the fact that it's your heart that is touched.

Growing,

Curt Iles
2004

Table of contents

The Wind in the Pines	1
Burned, yet Blessed, By the Fire	6
Branded!!!	13
A Father's Love	18
Rusty	28
A Jar Full of Marbles	35
Watch Out for the Fish	40
A $1000 Saddle on a $100 Horse	50
Whip-poor-will Day	53
A Song for the Wayfaring Stranger	59
Our Father Knows Best	62
Signs of the Sign Phantom 1974-1992	65
The Falcon	70
Uncle Quincy's Goose	72
A Wade in the River	79
Suzie Q	80
Can You Hear Me Now?	84
A Tale of Two Caps	88
The Heavenly Choir	96
Mr. Smith's Plane	105
Two Reasons Why I Believe in God	112
The Ripple Effect	118
"Trail Magic"	125
The Coach and the Ref	131
Available (but unused) Power	135
"Best Seat in the House"	138
Hey, Mr. Tambourine Man	142
The Mockingbird's Midnight Song	146
"Aunt Mary Jane"	149
A Soldier's Story	155
From Big D.C. to little d.c.	163
The Clear-Cut	169
Epilogue: "Happy and Sad"	176

x

The Wind in the Pines

A soft wind moving in the pines,
A mockingbird begins to sing,
A woman lullabies her child,
As evening spreads its wings.

Let nature sing, let nature sing.
A sweet harmony,
Never ending melody,
Let nature sing.

-Richard Betts
"Let Nature Sing"

As I begin this series of stories, it is dusk in Dry Creek, my hometown. I am at "The Old House," the spot where most of my stories are written. This log house, built by my ancestors at the end of the 19th century, is my favorite place on earth.

Sitting here, I can see the nearby woods as well as enjoy the sounds of the evening. The few birds of winter are chirping in the cedar trees of the front yard.

To the swamp side of the yard, I hear the scratching sound of a squirrel as it scampers up a Red Oak looking for a last acorn before settling down for the night. Looking up into the lofty tops of the pines, I see a faint breeze blowing through the limbs. The sound of the squirrel, the fading light, and the soft wind combine to give me a serene, peaceful feeling.

Wind in the Pines

I focus on the wind up in the pines. Well, in reality I'm keeping my eye on the movement of the limbs that shows the effects of the wind. You see, we cannot really see the wind, but we can see its effect as it passes through the tops of the trees on a cool evening.

Then I think back to a question often asked: "Curt, where do your stories come from?" It's a tough question that I never have an adequate answer to. My reply is usually, "Well, they just appear from everyday events and at the most unusual moments."

Numerous times I've pulled my truck to the side of the road and hurriedly scribbled out a story idea on a scrap of paper. I'm always afraid that to delay writing it down means I will lose the idea.

Today sitting on this porch, as I faintly hear the wind rustling in the tall pines, I'm struck by the idea of a story... this story... and as the ideas flow out, I begin writing.

Then I realize where my stories come from: they come softly from *the wind in the pines.* They often slip up on me quietly. If I'm not listening carefully, they may pass by unnoticed.

Writing this new story, I wonder how many great stories passed me by because I was too preoccupied to hear this wind in the pines.

The most important things in our lives can be easily overlooked due to their quiet nature. It is the chattering voices of the urgent and unimportant that often drown out the things that are truly most important.

I'm reminded of what is called, *"A father's most dangerous sentence"* – **"There is always tomorrow."**

It is so easy to miss the most important things in life by simply putting off people and events until later. Then we sadly learn that there is not always a tomorrow.

Looking at the wind in the tall Loblolly Pines between The Old House and the home of my parents, I recall my great grandparents and their stories of the virgin pine forests of Southwest Louisiana. Our area was blanketed with huge forests of Longleaf, or yellow pines as they were commonly called. They covered every acre except the creek bottoms and swamps where the hardwoods grew.

My ancestors told of towering pines that shut out the sunlight above. Due to this, no undergrowth or briars existed. Only a thick layer of pine straw carpeted the ground. My great grandmother "Doten" Iles told of how their wagon would ride quietly over the deep cushion of pine straw on the roads. She told of how a breeze always seemed to be blowing up high in the canopy of the limbs. She described this soft wind in the pines so vividly that I could nearly hear it in my seven year old mind.

Then the late 19th century and early years of the 20th century brought in the huge lumber companies that cut all the pines in an orgy of clear-cutting and greed.

The wind in the tall pines was no more. The sadness on Grandma Doten's face as she thought back to the virgin forests once surrounding her family homestead made me sad too. It is a sadness that stayed with me after she was gone.

Then the second half of the 20th century brought back the timber industry. First, the stumps of the once towering pines were dug, dynamited, and pushed out of the open fields. These stumps, still rich in turpentine, were processed and used in many products.

Then the modern forestry companies began what we call reforestation. They came back to these areas that had been barren of pines for decades and began planting pines.

These plantations became the new industry that now fuels our parish economy.

Most of our part of Louisiana is now covered with large stands of pines. The wind in the pines is heard once again. These wonderful tall trees, singing their soft song of nature as the wind moves their limbs, still move my heart.

Sitting here on the porch, darkness gradually settles in. Once again the wind dies down and the dominant sounds become the sounds of the night - crickets, frogs, owls, and coyotes.

Yes, my stories come from simple things, events, and the wonderful yet ordinary people who are my lifelong friends and neighbors.

I believe that God's quiet voice is very similar to the wind in the pines. His voice is so powerful, yet so easily ignored.

So as we begin this journey of another collection of stories- some humorous, a few sad, and all (hopefully) inspiring and joyous..... My prayer is that you'll hear *the wind in the pines.* And after hearing, you'll be more sensitive to the vast array of gifts around you that come directly from God.

That you'll step outside.... into nature, and even more importantly, step outside yourself, to see the richness of all that surrounds you.

My dream is that you'll be reminded that the things that matter in life, just like the wind in those pines, are often unnoticed and overlooked.

Life is really about things you can't "see"… love, family, and friendship. My book is about exactly the same thing – a celebration of those things "that we cannot see."

Hear the wind in your pines.
Gather your own stories.
Live richly the life of love you've been given by God.
May your heart (and mine) always hear this beautiful melody: this song of the wind in the pines.

Burned, yet Blessed, by the Fire...

A Longleaf Pine in the grassy straw stage.

Driving down Highway 113 toward the community of Reeves, I'm heartbroken by a scene on the west side of the road. A large field of Longleaf Pines has been the victim of a forest fire.

It must have been a hot fire because it completely burned the smaller trees and blackened the bark of the more mature trees up to over ten feet high. It's a sad sight to see acres of pines with blackened trunks and brown straw. It appears this entire stand will need to be re-planted.

But there is an amazing story behind the fire in the longleaf pines. Here it is: The history of the Longleaf Pine, *Pinus Palustrus* must be understood to truly grasp this story. This native tree, also called the yellow pine, ruled the virgin forests of the South from Virginia to East Texas.

Because of its hardiness, adaptability, and ability to grow in shallow, sandy soils, it covered much of the acreage of the southern United States

These beautiful pines existed in vast tracts called pine savannahs. These were upland areas where the pines were scattered throughout grassy areas. Because of the tall grasses, fire was always a reality during the dead of winter, when frost had killed the surrounding vegetation.

The first to burn the woods were the native Indians. They burned the savannahs to be able to see game animals better and lessen the chance of their enemies hiding nearby. Then later, white settlers burned these same grasslands to make better grazing for their cattle and sheep, as well as to kill pests such as redbugs and ticks.

No matter the reason for these fires, the Longleaf Pines continued to grow. Whereas non-native pines, such as Slash and Loblolly, are easily killed by wildfire, the Longleaf seems to thrive because of fire.

Looking at the charred trees along the Reeves-Dry Creek highway, I remembered how Longleaf Pines need fire to grow properly.

Longleaf Pine grows much slower than the other pine species. Because of that reason, most replanting of pines has favored the faster growing species, such as Loblolly or Slash pines.

The early stage of a Longleaf Pine is called the grassy stage. The tree has hardly any trunk above ground and the long green needles more nearly resemble a wild type of grass than a tree. The pine will stay in this "long straw" stage indefinitely until a fire sweeps through.

During this stage, the tree will remain dormant in growth due to what is called Brown Spot Needle Blight. This fungus attacks the top growth area of the young pine, called the candle bulb.

The combination of the tall grass around the tree competing for sunshine and nutrients, and the Needle Blight keeps the young pine tree from growing upward. The surrounding grass keeps the area moist, which is the condition the Needle Blight needs to attack the small pine's topmost candle bulb. The result is that the Longleaf sapling will stay in this grassy stage indefinitely - still alive, but never growing upward.

A Longleaf Pine will never reach its potential until a fire rushes through, killing the grass and other trees competing with it for water, sunlight, and nutrients. Additionally, the Brown Spot Needle Blight is killed by the heat of the fire. Now the bushy Longleaf Pine is freed by the fire to grow to its intended height and size...And doesn't a Longleaf grow tall and beautiful!

Curt Iles beside a large pine in Kisatchie National Forest

A few years ago I was hiking in the Kistachie National Forest area of Louisiana. This area, called "Red Dirt," is still populated by tall, thick stands of Longleaf pines. At the end of my hike, I hitched a ride with a forest ranger back toward my truck. We began talking about the beauty of the pines of Louisiana. He made a statement that is memorable,

"My daughter just got back from a vacation to twelve different states. She told me, 'Daddy, I saw lots of pretty sights and trees. But I didn't see anything more beautiful than the Kistachie Longleaf Pines of Louisiana.'"

I agree with her. I love those pines.

One of the reasons I love these pines is because of their resilience. Looking across the tract along the Reeves highway, I see pines of all sizes blackened and charred. The needles have been burned off the smaller trees, leaving a pitiful stump.

In the succeeding weeks, I inspect the field to see any new growth. Finally, in March the tops of the trees begin to show new green growth. Soon a healthy candle bulb, some nearly a foot long, begins to reach upwards. Over the coming weeks and months, this candle bulb turns into a tree trunk and sprouts fresh pine straw, and this once dwarfed Longleaf Pine will never again have to compete with the grass for water, sunlight, or food.

Knowing about this species, I also know that this same growth is taking place underground. If you've ever seen the exposed tap root of a Longleaf Pine, you know that it has a deep strong foundation for growth.

There is a spiritual application from the story about these pines. In our lives we need the fire of trials and challenges to grow into the person God wants us to be. None of us desire these times of heat and pain, but God uses these times for the shaping of our heart for maximum growth.

We see a memorable example of this "burned yet blessed" experience in the wonderful Old Testament story of Joseph. From Genesis chapters 37 through 41, Joseph endures continual hardship beginning with unjust betrayal by his own brothers. He is sold as a slave to a passing caravan, and then ends up in Egypt as a house slave.

Joseph is a young teenager in a foreign land but he retains his integrity and faith in the God of Israel in spite of serving as a slave in the house of Potiphar.

When he refuses the advances of his boss's wife (the evil Mrs. Potiphar) he is sent to prison in a frame-up worthy of any modern Hollywood movie. It seems as if anything Joseph does right results in punishment instead of reward. Even in prison his good deeds are forgotten by those who could help him gain freedom.

His thirteen year ordeal as a slave and prisoner ends one dramatic night when he is called before the Pharaoh of Egypt to interpret a troublesome dream. As Joseph interprets the dream, he carefully gives God the credit.

This amazing story continues as he is instantly promoted to Prime Minister by Pharaoh and oversees the preparation for a prophesied coming famine.

Then a few years later his brothers, who had betrayed him over two decades earlier, show up to buy food. Joseph has chance after chance to repay them for their evil deeds, but he exhibits no bitterness or hate in his heart.

Finally, revealing that he is really their long lost brother Joseph, he shows them total forgiveness and love. In chapter 50 of Genesis, Joseph makes one of the Bible's strongest statements, *"You intended to harm me, but God intended it for good to accomplish what is now being done: the saving of many lives."*

As Joseph looked back over the "burning fire" of slavery, betrayal, and prison he saw God's hand in each stage of his life, preparing him for divine service.

A brief study of the young Joseph in Genesis 37 reveals a spoiled bragging teenager. The "fires" of the succeeding years are what shapes him into the great height at which he stands as the savior of the families that will become the nation of Israel.

During these fiery times, we will often wonder where God is. Even though it is often difficult to feel His close presence in the fire, He is beside us as never before. It is good to be reminded of his faithfulness and steadfastness.

Later in the Bible the story of Shadrach, Meshach, and Abednego also illustrates these "blessings of being in the fire." The book of Daniel tells of these three young men being thrown into the fiery furnace for refusing to bow to the idolatry of the Babylonian king, Nebuchadnezzar.

The fire was so hot that it killed the soldiers tossing them in this furnace. Our three heroes were thrown in tightly bound, as good as dead.

In a few minutes the King and his advisors were amazed to see them walking around in the fire. His words tell the story better than we ever could:

"Look!" he answered, "I see four men loose, walking in the midst of the fire; and they are not hurt, and the form of the fourth is like the Son of God." (Daniel 3:25 NKJV)

In the fire, God did not desert them but showed up personally to stand by them. Also, in this fire "what bound them" was burned off. Just like the Longleaf's fungus blight, the hot fire burned off what was holding them back.

We all experience being in the fire at various times in our lives. None of us are exempt. Your fire will probably be much different from mine. Regardless, God wants to use this fire to shape you and use you. Throughout history the people God has used the most have been those who had worked through difficult circumstances to grow to their "maximum" height for use by Him.

Are you in the fire? If so, remember that God has not abandoned you. Just as Shadrach and his two partners were joined by God in the Babylonian fire, you are not alone.

And you can rest assured that your faithful Father is using this fiery trial to shape you and use you as never before.

If you are ever driving along La. 113 between Reeves and Dry Creek, take a look west at about mile marker 3. You'll see a field of Longleaf Pines of all sizes. Some are in neat rows while others are wild pines that have come up on their own.

And remember that these same pines have been burned by the hot fire. In fact they are purposely burned yearly for continued maximum growth. Looking at them, I hope you recall the story of how these Longleaf pines have been burned, yet blessed, by the fire.

Branded!!!

I came of age in the 1960's and early 70's. It was a time of great upheaval and change in America. I saw the events of this time one by one on TV - the assassinations and an unpopular war that brought down one president followed by the political underhandedness that brought down another.

We always laughed that in Southwestern Louisiana, the wild 60's didn't get to our area until the 70's. The age of long hair, rebellion, and rock music washed over our part of the state during my high school years. Looking back, it's still hard to believe that I once took part in a student strike that shut down our high school for two days... It was a strange time in history and I'm glad I was there to experience it.

The following story, from the early 1970's is one of my personal favorites. It was told to me by my great friend and college roommate, Terry "T-Bone" Perkins. It concerned an incident that happened with his uncle. Terry swore it really happened and it's just too good not to tell.

The Perkins family was longtime residents of the Pitkin area in Vernon Parish. It is a beautiful area of Louisiana dotted with small farms, country people, and miles of pine forests. The people of this area are good Folk - wonderful to have as friends and always ready to help.

However, the people of this area are not anyone to fool with. They are fearsome enemies when crossed. I learned this lesson clearly during my years as a basketball player and later as a coach. When you came into the Pitkin gym, you'd better be ready to play hard and fight your way out win or lose.

My story concerns four guys who could attest to the wisdom of leaving those Pitkinites alone.

Terry's uncle, Donald Perkins, was well known throughout our area because he operated the sale barn in DeRidder. For those of you not cultured, the sale barn was where weekly animal auctions took place. At Miller Brothers auction barn, this was always on Tuesday. The intersection of LA 26 and US 171, where the old sale barn was located, would always be crowded on Tuesdays with trucks and trailers and cowboys everywhere.

. . . And in the middle of this dusty noisy scene would always be Donald Perkins.

On the day of this particular story, Donald Perkins was traveling through Alexandria with a load of cattle. As usual he had on his cowboy hat, the truck window rolled down, and a big chew of Cotton Boll tobacco in his jaw. He tapped his brake as he approached a red light on Alexandria's main highway, Macarthur Drive.

As he came to a stop in the right northbound lane, he was joined by a car in the adjacent left lane. It was a loud Dodge Charger. Back then these powerful cars were called, "Muscle cars." Usually fueled by a large V-8 engine and a four barrel carburetor, they were full of power, painfully loud, and ready to roll.

Little did we know that these types of cars were dinosaurs being encountered by the coming ice age of the gas shortages of the mid-1970's. Their low gas mileage in the shadow of the long gas lines took these classics out of production.

In this particular red Dodge were four guys - not just any guys, but hippie guys. They were long haired, with scruffy beards, sporting sloppy clothes. The guy on the front passenger side wore a sleeveless cut off t-shirt and a smart aleck sneer as they pulled up beside the cattle truck.

Two distinct cultures were meeting side by side on the pavement of Macarthur Drive. There was definitely no love lost between these two opposite sides of dress, attitude, and values.

Because there were four of them, the hippies bravely began to make fun of the short red-faced cowboy sitting in the dented truck pulling the trailer load of lowing cattle. Their comments were slightly restrained, but Donald Perkins heard enough to know they were making fun of everything about him, his truck, and his load.

Fortunately the light turned green and the Dodge Charger, with its loud glass-packed dual exhausts, roared away. Donald and his loaded truck took off much slower.

As fate would have it, the next red light caught them both. As you can probably guess, they were once again side by side with three cars in front of each one. The Dodge arrived there ahead of the cattle truck, so the four hippies had plenty of time to get their one-line zingers ready for the cowboy. Since the previous red light, they had laughed enough about the cowboy that they felt free to direct their sarcastic remarks directly at Donald Perkins.

As I told you earlier, men from the Pitkin area are not the enemies you want, as these four hippies in the Charger were soon going to find out. By now he had heard enough, so Donald Perkins killed the engine on his truck and reached back behind him on his gun rack.

From the gun rack he pulled down a weapon....

But it wasn't a shotgun or rifle...Instead it was a cattle prod... Or what we call in our part of Louisiana, a "hotshot."

A hotshot is a thin pole about the length of a walking stick. On the pointed end it has two metal electrodes. When the end of this instrument is pushed against something that is conductive, a sharp jolt of electricity is given off.

The hotshot is a prime tool for any serious cattleman. It is effective in controlling and moving the biggest and most stubborn bull or cow. The jolt it gives does not cause injury or long term damage, but its shock will quickly and completely get the attention of even the rowdiest animal.

Now I know you're ahead of me on my story, so let's get back to Donald Perkins. He stepped out of the truck and approached the carload of rowdy animals. The guy on the front passenger side had his arm propped up on the door. Donald Perkins later related that when he stuck the guy in the armpit with his hotshot, "he bleated like a goat."

In quick succession he managed to stick all of them at least once. With all of the hollering, cussing, and scampering around, he wasn't sure, but thought he got the two on the passenger side a couple of times.

The Charger was fenced in by vehicles ahead, on both sides, as well behind, so there was no place for the car to escape. Just then, the light finally turned green, the cars ahead moved off, and the hippies in the Dodge sped off, probably not slowing down until they got across the Red River and into Pineville.

I've told and retold this story hundreds of times since the day "T-Bone" Terry Perkins acted it out in detail for me. Most of my stories have some spiritual lesson, but I'm not sure about this one. Well, I guess it's a lesson to keep your mouth shut and mind your own business, especially if you're parked next to a cowboy with a *loaded* gun rack.

Donald Perkins has been dead for many years now. But in my mind he is still alive - standing in the traffic lane of busy Macarthur Drive wielding his weapon like a skilled swordsman through the open windows of the hippie car.

...And probably somewhere in Rapides Parish, or maybe up in Pollock ... or down in Bunkie, some forty-something guy will read this story... and he'll feel a twinge of remembrance.... Maybe a sudden catch under his right arm, or a jolt in his memory, as he remembers that day on the four lane in Alexandria... when the crazy cowboy attacked him and his buddies with that strange instrument that stung.

Yes, he'll remember that day... forever "branded" in his mind... when he was stuck by the hotshot from the short cowboy from Pitkin... ("That's Pitkin, Louisiana, boy... And when you say it, say it with respect) ...where the men are strong, the women are all beautiful, and you don't make fun of a man's cowboy hat, his truck, his cows, or his chew of tobacco.

"A Father's Love"

It's graduation night at our high school. My wife DeDe and I are sitting in the reserved seating section at the football stadium. Our son Clint is graduating tonight and it is a very special night. Most of the fifty plus graduates who'll march across the stage have traveled throughout their school journey together. It's hard to believe that thirteen years ago they were in Kindergarten and I was watching many of them play T-ball.

I always feel sorry for kids who don't get to attend a K-12 school. To start school with a group and finish twelfth grade with most of them creates a special bond among students. They know each other as well as their teachers. Due to this, they hold a special camaraderie that urban students can never quite understand.

We've settled in and gotten comfortable in our chairs down on the track. I look around for our principal Mr. Cooley. Graduation night is one of the most stressful nights for a high school principal. As a former school administrator, you never know what a student, parent, or visitor may do on this night of celebration and success.

I've seen or heard of it all - senior boys coming by, one by one, putting a pebble in the principal's palm as he shakes their hand and presents their diploma. The principal must keep stopping and putting the pebbles down to perform the ceremonial duties of handing out the diplomas.

Then there are the loudmouths who will wait until that "pregnant pause" in the ceremony and holler out something. Two years ago at my oldest son Clay's graduation, a fellow graduate named Chad walked up to receive his diploma. It was a Kodak moment because Chad had labored a long time to get on this stage. A smattering of surprised applause broke out when his name was mentioned. Most of us had never expected to see him walk across this stage. We were all happy and I thought about how many teachers and adults had pushed, taught, and begged to get Chad to this moment.

Just as he was handed his diploma, someone way up in the stadium with good lungs hollered,

"Run, Chad, run before they take it back!"

Even the principal had to laugh at that.

So sitting here as an ex-principal, I can relax and enjoy the night. My only concern is that Clint is making a speech and I have no idea what he'll say. But I'm confident our man will do just fine.

It's now about fifteen minutes before the ceremony begins. I look behind me to see the stands filling up. There is a murmur of anticipation throughout the crowd on this beautiful May evening.

That's when I first see him.... A man in a cowboy hat strides to the podium on stage. Removing his hat, he leans into the microphone and blows on it. Yes, it's on... and he literally has the stage to himself, as well as the mike. Most people haven't even noticed him. I look around for Mr. Cooley, but don't see him anywhere near. For the thousandth time since I left the school ten years ago, I'm glad I'm no longer a principal.

Then our man at the mike begins to sing. With no accompaniment he sings,

"Son, let me tell you about a father's love,
A secret that my father said was between just us.

*You see, Daddies don't just love their children
every now and then,
It's a love without end, Amen.
It's a love without end, Amen."*

I faintly recognize the tune and remember it – It's the chorus of a George Strait song entitled, *"A Father's Love."*

Then about the same time, I recognize the singer on stage - it's Greg Fontenot. Greg's son David is graduating tonight. David is a favorite of all of us - a wonderful smile and winning personality, an excellent athlete as well as a good student.

Although I don't know Mr. Fontenot extremely well, I've always enjoyed visiting with him. He is an expert in a trade that always brings respect in rural areas- he is an excellent welder. He is also a true country man as evidenced by the fact that on the side of his welding truck is painted,

"I ain't J.R. and this ain't Dallas...
But I can sure plow, plant, and hoe.
...and God bless."

By now Mr. Fontenot is singing the first stanza. He has now captured the attention of most of the crowd. Glancing around, some are sniggering; others sit in gape-jawed wonder. Someone behind me says, "I believe he's drunk." But watching closely, I can tell that Greg's not drunk, he's just singing a George Strait song from his heart.

*I got sent home from school one day
with a shiner on my eye.*

*Fighting was against the rules and
it didn't matter why.
When dad got home I told that story
just like I'd rehearsed,
then stood on those trembling knees,
expecting the very worst...*

*...and he said,
Son, let me tell you about a father's love,
A secret that my father said was between just us.
You see, Daddies don't just love their children
every now and then; It's a love without end, Amen.
It's a love without end, Amen.*

And Mr. Fontenot is singing this song well, which is not easily done acapella. He has a fine country singing voice that does justice to this song. As Greg Fontenot begins the second verse, it is very evident that he has practiced and prepared for this night a long time. He continues,

*When I became a father in the spring of '81,
There was no doubt that stubborn boy
was just like my father's son.
When I thought my patience had been tested to the
end, I took my daddy's secret and passed it on to him.*

This time when he gets to the chorus, I hear a few voices in the large crowd join in:
"It's a love without end, amen."

By now I'm thinking to myself, I bet David is dying of embarrassment and wanting to hide. I think about my own three boys and remember the cardinal rule of raising teenagers: *"Don't embarrass me in front of my friends."*

When Greg finishes the second stanza, he pauses and spits into a bottle he is holding. I think to myself that I'd need a lot more than a dip of Skoal to have the courage to stand on a stage and do what he's doing.

Then, just as he begins the third and climatic stanza, someone cuts off the microphone. I'm sitting close enough to hear him exclaim, "Dang, if they didn't cut me off."

Someone sitting near us says, "Well, they should have let him go ahead and finish it if they'd let him sing that much." Another local music critic adds, "He was really doing pretty good and by the way, that third verse is the best one." A smattering of applause comes from the audience, mixed in with many good hearted shouts, and a few whistles.

Greg Fontenot stands there as if they'll turn back on the microphone if he just waits long enough. After what seems an eternity, but really is only ten seconds or so, he walks down the stage steps onto the playing field.

. . .Now, what happens next is why this is such a memorable story:

From across the field, where the graduates are assembled, comes a flash. It is a student running with his robe trailing behind him. He is holding onto his cap as he sprints.

You've probably guessed who it is running across the field - it's David Fontenot, running full tilt toward his dad.

He's running across the same field where last fall, wearing number 80, he ran so many times with the football.

He runs up to his dad and embraces him warmly. I can read his lips repeating, "Thank you, thank you," over and over. I now realize we have seen a special gift from a father to his son. An act from a father that will help "weld" their souls together for the rest of their lives.

I realize that this country father understands about more than one type of welding- and I'm not talking about metal or welding rods - but a welding of the human heart.

Only later do I learn that Greg Fontenot had been planning this song all year. He had even asked the principal to allow him to sing before the ceremony started. Mr. Cooley had kind of put him off and probably forgot about it until on graduation night when Greg sang his first solo.

During the coming days, I enjoyed sharing the story of David and his dad. I also began thinking of all of the many ways a man can give his "blessing" to a son or daughter.

In the Bible we see this in several stories. Each one unique but conferring the same story, "You are my child and I see something very special in you. I am proud of you."

By far the most powerful Biblical example of a father's blessing is at Jesus' baptism. As Jesus begins his public ministry at age thirty, he chooses to be baptized in the Jordan River by his older and more well-known cousin, John.

Jesus, being the perfect Son of God, did not need baptism for repentance of sins- because He was sinless. He sought baptism as an example of obedience. John the Baptist even initially refused to baptize Jesus, famously stating that he was not worthy to even untie Jesus' sandals.

After John relented and the newly baptized Christ came up out of the water, the scriptures state, "The Holy Spirit came down like a dove and a loud voice spoke from Heaven:
'This is my beloved Son in whom I am well pleased."

The statement above was one of a father blessing His son. Jesus needed to hear that from His Father. Jesus, being perfect and having existed with God from before eternity, still needed those words of approval.

The excellent book, *The Blessing* by John Trent, shares numerous accounts of the importance of fathers and their words and actions of approval and blessing on their children.

I started thinking about my own father and how he gave "the blessing" to me. My father came from a very good family. However, they weren't much on flowery words or saying, "I love you." Because of that he was never really comfortable sharing, "I love you." with us. But I never felt shortchanged one bit. There was never one moment in my life where I ever doubted the love of both my mom and dad for me.

Daddy had many ways to say, "I'm pleased and proud of you." Here are a few ways that I cherish:

When I was a young Christian in high school, I led one of my friends, Jimmy, to the Lord. Next week at our church youth meeting, Daddy asked me to tell the story about how it happened in, of all places, the parking lot of the Sugar Bowl Skating Rink. He let me know that he was proud of my spiritual growth. God used that to continue to fan the flames of my young love affair with Jesus.

My dad was a tremendous athlete. One of the joys of my life was playing on the same softball team with him. In his prime years, up through age forty, Daddy was the finest leftfielder you've ever seen. He could cover some ground and made many fabulous catches throughout our years of playing beside each other in the outfield.

Sometime in his forties he moved in to pitch and leftfield became my spot. I enjoyed the challenge and opportunity. I'd had many good lessons on how to play this position that my dad excelled at.

Once we were playing and a guy hit a long fly way over my head. As I sprinted back I turned the wrong way and saw the ball was going over my other shoulder. I attempted to awkwardly turn around and adjust. Twisted like this I just threw my glove up over my shoulder. The sweet thud of the ball landing in my glove surprised me way more than it did anyone else watching.

When I came in to the dugout, Daddy simply said, "That was the catch of all catches." That simple statement meant more to me than if I'd been on the cover of *Sports Illustrated* or on that night's ESPN top ten. My dad was giving me his blessing - and it came in an area that was very special to both of us. You see, the best parental blessings always take place in an area of shared love and passion.

I became camp manager at Dry Creek when I was thirty-six. Not too long after that a friend came up to me and related, "I was at a meeting where your dad sang. He introduced himself as 'Curt's father' and called you 'his hero.'"

Over and over during the last decade of his life he would say that about me. Many times he said it in front of me. Words cannot describe how much it meant to me. It amazed me that the man who was always *my* hero thought of me as *his*. That motivated me, and still does, to be the father, husband, and man I should be.

Here's a final thing about my dad's "blessings"- It released me from ever feeling like I had to be just exactly like him.

Since his death a year ago, I've heard repeatedly, "Son, you've got some big shoes to fill." I always smile and agree with them. But I've never felt like I must fill my dad's shoes. As great of a man as he was, he gave me the freedom to be my own man- allowing me to make my own decisions and choose my own path.

That's one of the things about the blessing - it brings freedom and release.

Yes, the blessing...
Coming from a father's love....
It's priceless.....

Finally, Greg Fontenot's graduation song, which really started off this long spiel, had a wonderful third verse. Even though Greg never got to sing it on that May night, it bears repeating. It tells of the best blessing of all, our Heavenly Father's love for us:

Last night I dreamed I'd died and stood
Before those pearly gates,
When suddenly I realized there must
be some mistake.
If they know half of the things I've done
they'll never let me in.
Then somewhere from the other side I
heard these words again,

And He said,
"Son, let me tell you about a father's love,
A secret that my father said was between just us.
You see, Daddies don't just love their children every now and then,
It's a love without end, Amen.

　　　　　…Yes, it's a love without end, Amen.
　　　　　　A love without end,
　　　　　　　　　　　Amen.

"A Father's Love"
Copyright by George Straight

Rusty

Rusty Thompson on the highway

As I'm walking down the road to the camp entrance, I look at the intersection that serves as the center of Dry Creek community and I see him... There he comes... He's walking down the middle stripe of Highway 113. It's Beauregard parish's most recognizable citizen - Rusty Thompson.

Behind Rusty comes a work group of inmates clad in orange jumpsuits. They are cleaning the roadside ditches of trash. Accompanying this human caravan is a prison van and DOTD dump truck, both flashing their amber caution lights.

It's the closest thing we've seen to a parade here in Dry Creek, and there is no doubt who the drum major of this parade is. It's Rusty Thompson.

He's wearing his old tan jumpsuit with an orange vest completing his wardrobe. He wears a baseball cap cocked on the side of his head and rhythmically waves an orange caution flag. In his front vest pocket is an empty styrofoam cup, ready to fill with coffee if someone offers some.

To say that Rusty Thompson is walking would be a gross understatement of his gait. I would say he is high-stepping it ahead of everyone else. His unusual gait, location and style cause me to flash back to the Grambling State University band. I once saw them perform and their drum major moved a lot like Rusty: loosely stepping out, every limb grooving in an impossibly different direction.

There may be a sergeant in the van and a driver in the truck, but this is Rusty's work crew and he is leading it well.

After talking with Rusty on the roadway, I invite the whole crew back to the camp for lunch, to which they readily agree.

As Rusty and his entourage pass by, I tell Jake, one of our younger workers, "That man right there is Rusty Thompson, the most well-known man in Beauregard Parish."

You could stop at Super Wal-Mart in DeRidder and ask the average shopper if they know who Gerald Johnson is; they might know what the mayor of DeRidder looks like. Others might recognize our state senator, James David Cain, if they saw him. But I'm confident many more would nod their head and smile to the question, "Do you know Rusty Thompson?"

There are all kinds of reasons why folks know Rusty. The biggest one is that he is a man of the road. Rusty has worked for the Highway Dept. for over 25 years. During this time and throughout his entire life he has never driven or owned a car. I've always found it ironic that a lifetime highway worker has never owned a car, but with Rusty Thompson a lot of things are ironic and thought-provoking.

So Rusty's mode of transportation has always been his feet or rather his thumb. He is our area's most well known hitchhiker. That is how he gets to work, church, ballgames, shopping and even courting. He once had me drop him off at a "woman friend's" house who was cooking supper for him.

Many times I have topped a hill on Louisiana 394 or U.S. 171 and seen a silhouetted figure way ahead on the road shoulder. Long before I could make out any features, I would confidently know it was Rusty. No other human being could naturally stand in the posture of Rusty: feet spread out, head cocked, and right thumb sticking out.

Many people in our area have Rusty Thompson hitchhiking stories. I've heard many variations on this basic story:

"We were going to a basketball game in Opelousas and we passed Rusty on the highway. When we walked in the gym two hours later he was already there, sitting in the bleachers and eating a bag of popcorn."

My favorite Rusty hitchhiking tale is one I've never been able to get him to admit or deny:

Years ago a Dry Creek native was getting married in the north Louisiana town of Jonesboro. Rusty caught a series of rides to arrive just before the wedding. He did not want to miss out on this social event. After the wedding was over and the reception ended, Rusty knew he needed to get a ride south.

Fortunately he had overheard that the groom and bride would be honeymooning in Beaumont, Texas. Sure enough, he bummed a ride with the newlyweds and got them to drop him off when they went through DeRidder.

I hope it doesn't seem like I'm making fun at Rusty's expense. He will laugh the hardest when he reads this story. He is a man who loves to tease, tell stories, and just enjoy being around folks.

To some, Rusty might seem simple but don't underestimate his mind. He is a genius with figures and numbers. Years ago, older boys would tell about his calculations in the watermelon fields. He could figure all types of amounts, weights, and distances.

He also possesses a phenomenal memory. A few years ago he told my wife, "DeDe, you played on that Harrisonburg 1972 state championship basketball team that beat East Beauregard 36-19." I went home and looked in an old yearbook, and sure enough there was the score, exactly as Rusty has recalled it.

He also is a whiz with names and knows everyone. He can also trace most family's ancestry back several generations. I always encourage teenage couples who are in love to avoid Rusty. He will go back into your family trees and figure out some way that the two lovebirds are kin to each other.

Rusty loves to sing. One interesting thing is when he sings a song containing every book of the Bible. It is a song he personally composed. What he may have lacked in talent was more than compensated by his enthusiasm.

Rusty is also a good writer. Several times he has written very articulate letters to the editor on local political or social issues.

About 1969 Rusty began refereeing basketball. I was amazed that he could pass the vision portion of the test, if there is one, because he was hit by at least two cars.

Rusty was at his best as a basketball official. He loved the game, knew nearly everyone in the gyms, and just looked like he was enjoying himself. Consistent with his personality, every call was made with great dramatic flair.

And for some reason most fans and coaches cut him slack when bad calls were made, which were numerous. However, I did hear once that a family he rode to the game with refused to let him ride back because of a game-ending controversial call that Rusty made against their team.

John Rudd, a DeRidder native who went on to play for the New York Knicks in the NBA, told me of one on-court experience with Rusty.

He related that a loose ball scuffle under the goal brought a whistle from Rusty. John swears that Rusty spun around and dramatically pointed at him for the foul. "Foul on 00 for hacking on the arm."

John said he was standing far away from the loose ball. He said Rusty whirled as if he was doing a dance step before pointing him out.

But my favorite Rusty refereeing story is one I witnessed in about 1970. East Beauregard was playing Elizabeth in the East Beauregard High gym. This was just before integration began in schools.

Elizabeth had a fine basketball player named Charles Robinson. He was a member of the only black family in Elizabeth. He was a fine ball player and went by the nickname of "Shine."

Rusty was refereeing this game, which E.B. was winning easily. Due to the lopsided score the student section had become bored and needed something to excite them.

Some smart aleck student started yelling "Throw the ball to Snowball." Of course this ignorance was directed at Charles Robinson, who was probably the first black player to play in E.B.'s gym.

This went on for a few trips up and down the court. I kept waiting for a principal or teacher to come over and stop the shenanigans from the bleachers.

However, there was no need for anyone else to stop the catcalls because Rusty took charge. He waved his arms as he shrilly blew his whistle. Rusty turned toward the student section as the crowd suddenly quieted.

It got as quiet as a bunch of Quakers at a love feast. Then Rusty wailed out as he indicted the entire student section:

"Technical on you...for calling him 'Snowball!'"

All I remember is how the quiet crowd exploded in laughter and guffaws. Even the Elizabeth players, including Charles Robinson, were doubled over laughing and shaking their heads.

Not long after the infamous snowball game is when Rusty retired and officially hung up his whistle.

But in reality Rusty was still a referee at heart. He now took up his permanent place of honor against the wall on the east end of the gym. Today if you attend a game at our school, you will see him leaning against the cinderblock wall. From this vantage point he helps the black and white striped "officials" call the game.

During my years of coaching basketball, I would often look at Rusty to see if he agreed with a call under "his basket."

I especially enjoyed seeing Rusty's reaction to basketball's toughest call - whether player contact was a charge or blocking foul.

I'd look down that end of the court where the "real" referee signaled a blocking foul on the defensive player. Rusty would sadly shake his head as he dramatically made the opposite signal for a charging foul, just steps away from the referee. I would elbow Coach Larry Greene and say, "I don't know if that call was right, but Rusty sure didn't agree with it."

Another reason why I love Rusty is due to his fine Christian character. I've never known Rusty Thompson to use bad language or tell an off-color joke. His humor of just being himself is way more effective than what any obscene word or story could add. He is a man who loves God and is never ashamed to tell about it.

I close with one final Rusty story:

Once a Beauregard Parish couple went to Rome on vacation. On Sunday they decided to visit the Vatican for a papal appearance. They were part of a huge crowd that was assembled in St. Peter's Square for the pope's appearance. Right on time, the pope came out onto the balcony. Beside him stood another man.

The Americans stood there, pointed and asked a nearby Italian, "Who is that other guy up there?" The Italian answered without hesitation, "I don't know who the guy in the tall white hat is, but that's Rusty Thompson up there on the left."

You and I both know this story from Rome is not true, but knowing Rusty Thompson, only a few weeks in Italy would probably make it so.

A Jar Full of Marbles

I go to the cemetery - a place I visit often while helping family members select gravesites. It is always a very sobering job to stand with others at this place of tears and grief. Being here is a ministry as well as a labor of love. It is a great open window for caring in the name of Jesus. This is an unchangeable truth - *People who've lost a loved one are always ready for a kind word, hug, and a heartfelt prayer.*

Usually when meeting a person or family here, we'll walk out into the cemetery to select their spot. However, today I'm not waiting to meet anyone else. I'm here alone in the early morning quietness of Dry Creek Cemetery.

Today I'm marking the grave I've dreaded - the burial spot of my dad. He died yesterday after a courageous two-year battle with cancer. In my hand I hold the grave marker from Hixson's Funeral Home. It is difficult to believe that this marker, which I've driven in the ground dozens of times, will now be placed at the grave of my father.

I go to our family plot, and using my measuring tape select dad's gravesite near the graves of my grandparents. As I measure, the quietness of the cemetery is both comforting and unsettling. So many emotions are running through my mind and heart. But there is one strong feeling that eclipse all of them - an unexplainable feeling of peace... coupled with a deep sense of thankfulness.

I miss my dad so much already, but I'm full of gratitude that I had him as my friend and role model for my forty-six years. I'm thankful for the faithful life he lived for God, my mom, and our family. He finished strong... and he finished well.

. . . Because of that, I'm filled with a "happy sorrow." The tears come and go, but they are a mix of quiet joy as well as grief. I recall the words of Paul in I Thessalonians 4:13,

"...or to grieve like the rest of men, who have no hope."

I have hope... the assurance of eternity and life. After marking dad's grave I walk through the center of the cemetery. I go by the oldest section of graves near the old dying cedar tree. It is well over one hundred years old and marks the spot of the first burial here in 1880. I walk by the grave of my great-great-great grandmother, Nancy Wagnon. She and her husband, Andrew Jackson Wagnon, left their families in Georgia and came to this area in the 1840's. She is buried alone. Her husband, Grandpa Wagnon, was one of the many men who left their homes to fight in the Civil War and never returned.

Walking westward, I near the grave I want to see on this morning - the grave of my dear friend Ricky Gallien. Ricky died last September after a struggle with another dangerous and potentially fatal disease - depression. As I stand at the foot of his grave, sorrow sweeps over me once again. But that sorrow is once again tempered with quiet peace.

It has been eight months since Ricky's death at his own hands. Although the pain and confusion of the loss still cuts deeply, God is giving me the great gift He gives us when we grieve - The reminders of the joys of lifetime friendship, growing up together, worshipping God together, funny stories of Ricky's rich life, and how he loved his wonderful family and many friends.

The peace of God's word, where I always go for comfort and assurance, comes to me. I recall Ricky's favorite verse: Romans 8:28. This verse will adorn his tombstone when it is placed here. It is a "rock solid" verse that has comforted "Godly grievers" for two thousand years:
"And we know that in all things God works for the good of those who love Him, who have been called according to His purpose."

Yes, I've seen much good occur since that sad September day, even in the midst of unbelievable grief over Ricky's death. I have the peaceful knowledge that our God is continuing to bring good out of the most heartbreaking thing we've experienced.

Promises like Romans 8:28 are a wonderful gift from God. We are reminded that God's grace, mixed with the steady progression of time, allows us to vividly remember the joyful times and relationships while at the same time soothing the hurtful emotions. In no way am I inferring that the searing pain ever goes away. It is too deep and personal for that to occur. However, our faithful God places His strong hand on the hurt and gives us the grace to go on.

I kneel beside Ricky's grave. I'm reminded that if he was alive, he would be preaching my dad's funeral tomorrow. And I remember how much I loved Ricky and how I miss him, and how I'm going to miss my dad in the same way. My dad was a father figure to Ricky and many other young men in Dry Creek. Daddy and Ricky had a special relationship that was tied securely in their similar interests, hobbies, and passion for God.

I pick up a faded orange Houston Astros cap lying by Ricky's grave. It's a gift left here in Ricky's memory. My dad, Ricky, and I shared a love of the Astros and suffered and celebrated with them all of these years. I think about so many fun trips to the Astrodome with dad and our family. I smile as I think about the times Ricky, his brother Mike, and others of us went to watch an entire weekend series. You talk about country come to town!

I place the cap back by his grave. One more time I tell him that "our Astros" will one day win the World Series and I'll come down here to celebrate. Now that Daddy's grave is also here, I'll have another faithful fan to visit with.

Setting the faded cap down, I reach for the real reason I wanted to come by Ricky's grave before heading home. I just wanted to count the marbles in the jar...

Ricky's only daughter, Kristi, plays basketball at Louisiana College. Ricky was so proud of her and they shared that very special love that exists between a dad and his daughter. When Kristi began her basketball season shortly after her dad's death, the coach gave each girl on the team a handful of marbles.

To the seniors she gave twenty-four marbles, juniors – like Kristi - got forty-eight. Coach McIntosh told the girls, "These marbles represent how many basketball games you have left in your career. After each game I want you to do something special with one of the marbles."

You can probably guess what Kristi has done with each marble. There at her dad's grave is a simple mason fruit jar. Beginning in the fall, and on into the winter, the jar has slowly filled up with marbles... and the sweet heartfelt notes left by a special daughter. Their season is now over. It will be next November before the jar continues to be filled. I pick up the pint jar of marbles and realize I am holding a very precious treasure in my hand. I dare not open it or read the enclosed notes. It is enough for me to simply touch it and realize what it means.

I turn to leave and make my way back to the truck. Once again, I go by dad's spot. Stopping, I am reminded that this is where his earthly body, the physical part that I will always identify with my father, will be laid to rest tomorrow. The human body that my mom, sisters, and I watched breathe his last breath yesterday, will be laid to rest right here.

But the "real Clayton Iles," that God-breathed soul the Creator puts in my dad, now lives on.
...And already, less than twenty-four hours after his death, God is sharing His wonderful gift of grace with me: The mental picture of my dad in these last weeks - old, sick, and feeble, are being washed away by the memories of the "wondrously alive" man I called Daddy - The lover of games, the man of a thousand witty sayings, the bass singer, the constant whistler, the great teacher, and the loving man who was deeply loved in return by all.

I guess I could put it this way: God is filling up my jar. And He's filling it up with the beautiful marbles of those happy memories. I recall the wise words of my special friend, Mrs. Helyn Aguillard:

"Now you must cash in on your wonderful memories -
They are like money in the bank -
except they never run out.
They pay such wonderful interest,
even when you are sad."

Yes, just like money in the bank . . .Or marbles in the jar. Those wonderful, wonderful memories that are God's special gift of grace to all of us.

Watch out for the Fish

It's real popular now to put a Christian fish on the bumper of your car. It is a replica of the simple two-mark symbol used as a secret code by the Christians of the first century.

The "fish on car" sends a message that the person behind the wheel is, hopefully, a Christian. But it is also scary - the responsibility that other drivers around us are going to watch closely to see if our driving habits model the teachings of Jesus.

I recall the popular bumper sticker of my teen years, "Honk, if you love Jesus!" I heard the story of one happy Christian carload that kept honking at the bumper stickered Ford LTD in front of them. Their honking brought no reply until finally the driver put his arm out the window and gave an obscene gesture that is definitely not associated with Jesus.

The Ford driver had either stolen the car (hopefully), forgotten his message (probably), or just didn't really give a care. (possibly)

The same is true with the fish. We should be very careful in wearing or exhibiting any symbol representing Christ unless our corresponding actions will bring Him glory, and not embarrassment.

We've all seen examples of fish-adorned cars driving aggressively or refusing to let someone into traffic. This is a poor witness and will never draw others to Jesus.

Before I get too spiritual, I must admit that I've stopped to check out my shirt before leaving work to go to a little league baseball game. At summer camp, we all wear coordinated color shirts with the camp logo on front and an appropriate scripture on the back.

I've thought, "I'd better behave if I'm going to sit in front of someone and holler at that blind umpire wearing "For me to live is Christ" on my back.

What I realize is that folks see "a verse" on my back whether I'm wearing an orange Dry Creek shirt or not. They know I claim to be a Christian... The sobering question is whether or not my actions and words match up with my beliefs.

The famous Indian leader Gandhi spent a major portion of his life studying the teachings of Jesus Christ. Gandhi, a Hindu, was once asked why he did not become a Christian. His reply should cut to our hearts: I'll become a Christian when I see one."

None of us can approach the sinlessness and Godliness of Jesus Christ, but that is no excuse for us to be sloppy in our behavior, words, and attitudes. We can draw others to Jesus or drive them away....

...And that brings me to one of my favorite stories on this subject:

A few summers ago Clay, my nephew Adam, and I made a hiking trip to the Smoky Mountains of Tennessee. We had a great time walking and enjoying the beauty of this special part of our Eastern mountains. Most of our hiking was on a section of the famous Appalachian Trail. The AT, as it is commonly known, runs for over 2000 miles from Georgia to Maine.

The boys, both in college at the time, were good hikers and I had some difficulty keeping pace with their youthful legs. After about four days of walking, I could sense that they were ready to return to civilization... and their girlfriends. In reality I was ready for home too.

So we made a deal: if it either started raining or we encountered a bear, we would end this great trip and begin our homeward trek. One of my goals on this trip was for the boys to see a bear in the wild. On previous hikes I'd seen several on this very section of the trail.

On our fourth night out, both the bear and the rain came. At dusk as we finished supper I sent the boys to wash our pots. Quickly they came running hollering out of the dark. They'd encountered a pretty large bear. It was evident it was following them back from the sound in the nearby bushes.

I turned my flashlight on him and saw movement. It was a good sized black bear. I used my loudest coach's voice to scare him off, but it did not deter him from coming on toward our campsite.

The bear turned and went behind the rock shelter and came even closer. It was evident Mr. Bear had lost his fear of humans and acquired a taste for granola bars and peanut butter.

I picked up a shovel from the shelter and waved it menacingly. The boys were quickly gathering our cooking gear and bags to put inside the wire-enclosed shelter.

A Smoky Mountain AT shelter is constructed the very opposite of a zoo - The humans are enclosed and the animals (bears, skunks, porcupines, and deer) come to look in.

*A Smoky Mountain National Park trail shelter.
(Notice the wire fence and gate to keep the bears out.)*

    The three of us got in the shelter, closed the gate, and collapsed in a loud fit of laughter and excitement as the bear moved about nosily in the nearby darkness.   One of the two brave hearts with me finally said, "Well, can we go home now?"
    It began raining during the night and the next morning, none worse for the wear, we hiked out the last five miles in the rain. That was a good way to end a memorable hiking trip.
    We began our 800 mile drive home, full of good stories and experiences. Everything went fine until the

Alabama-Mississippi state line. Just as we approached an I-20 exit for Toomsuba Mississippi, it sounded as if the van had run over a land mine. There was clanking and a loud thumping underneath the van that could only be bad news.

Fortunately we were right at this exit and eased off the interstate and into the parking lot of a convenience store. Revving the engine in gear, nothing happened. Looking under the van where the noise had been loudest, it was evident our drive shaft was gone.

We went in the store and asked the one clerk behind the counter, "What would a fellow do in Toomsuba if his car broke down late on Saturday afternoon?" He hardly looked up from his newspaper as he commented,

"Get a motel room until Monday."

I said, "Well, sir we can't do that. Surely there's someone around here that can work on a vehicle now."

He sat there a while looking at me and finally said, "Well, Bunyard's junkyard is down the road. Let me call and see if they're home."

Happily for us, he got an answer. From my end of the conversation I could tell that they were leaving soon for the stock car races, but would come by and at least look at it.

Within minutes an old red pickup pulled up. Two men got out. It was my first, but not last, time to meet James Bunyard and his son Al. Mr. Bunyard looked to be in his 60's and Al was probably half that age. While Al crawled under the van, his dad listened to my sad plight of being stranded 350 miles from home. Al scooted out and said, "We might have one for it back at the yard." I could tell they were in a hurry and thanked them profusely as they drove off.

While waiting I thought, "What will we do if they don't have the part?" Fortunately though, they soon returned with a drive shaft hanging out of the truck bed. Mr. Bunyard said, "I think this one will work." Al quickly slid under the van and began attaching the shaft. Clay whispered that Al did most of the work with one hand as his other hand carefully held a burning cigarette.

I attempted to make small talk with Mr. Bunyard but realized he was a man of few words and really didn't care to talk too much with a stranger. So I shut up and was just thankful they were willing to help. I also silently thanked the Lord that we broke down right where an exit and help were available.

Al finished his one-handed task and slid back out. He got into the van and drove it across the parking lot. Once again, we were ready to go.

I had already told the boys that we'd have to figure out about how to pay. I had no idea what the parts or labor would be. I was just thankful for their help and willing to pay any reasonable amount.

I asked, "Mr. Bunyard, what do I owe you?" He shuffled his feet and said, "Well, the drive shaft is $100. You can pay whatever you want on our labor." I replied, "Would you be happy with $150 total?" He said that he would be very satisfied with that amount.

Next came the statement that I was most concerned about: "Mr. Bunyard, I don't have that much cash. Do you take credit cards?" He quickly stated that he did not take cards.

Carefully, I said, "Will you be willing to take a check from me?" Anyone in business knows the danger of taking personal checks, especially from strangers out of state. His tone was much cooler toward me as he said, "I don't like taking checks - especially from people I don't know. I've been burned too many times."

I told him that although he didn't know me, he could trust me. I assured him that I sure wasn't going to cheat him with my son and nephew standing there. He snorted as if he'd heard every sorry excuse ever made for non- payment.

Before they had come back with the part I had prepared for this moment. I'd got out a copy of my first book, *Stories from the Creekbank*. I placed my business card in it.

It was at this uncomfortable point in the payment discussion that I proudly handed the skeptical Mr. Bunyard the book. He glanced at it and quickly back at me as if he was mentally trying to figure out what type of con artist I was.

It was then that I made my major mistake. I pulled my business card out of the book and handed it to him. It read:

DRY CREEK
BAPTIST CAMP

CURT ILES
Manager

P.O. Box 445
Dry Creek, LA 70637

Office (318) 328-7531
Home (318) 328-7215
E-mail: dcbcamp@aol.com

I told him with a smile, "Mr. Bunyard, I'm one of those good Baptists. You know I wouldn't cheat you."

With that statement, he became very animated and agitated. "Yes, I know all about you 'good Baptists.' Last year a fellow broke down on the interstate and I replaced his transmission. He told me he was a Baptist preacher from Birmingham and would pay me on his next trip through. As you can probably guess, I'm still waiting."

James Bunyard was now working up a good head of steam. "I'll tell you something else. I'll be waiting for him to pay for that transmission a year from now too! Well, I guess I'll have to take your check, but I don't want to and besides, I'm not sure I trust you."

I stood as straight as I could and shot back, "You may have been cheated before, but you won't be this time, you can rest assured on that!" I was getting a little passionate myself.

He was shorter than me but he got right up near my face and pointed a calloused finger. "Just remember This - what goes around comes around and if you cheat me, it will come back on you sooner or later."

I was very happy to agree with his statement because it is an accurate one. I handed him the check from City Savings Bank in DeRidder, Louisiana. He looked at it as if I'd just given him 150 Confederate dollars. We shook hands and they left in their truck for the races as we resumed our westward trek on I-20.

During our conference, Al, Adam, and Clay had all stood quietly. When we got back on the road, the boys began to have a good time with it. "Uncle Curt, he sure got worked up when you told him you were a Baptist," Adam laughed. I was quick to agree that my "Baptist ID" was probably not a good idea.

The next week I called the bank and found that the Bunyard check had cleared. I also wrote James and Al a note thanking them for their rescue, promising to stop in at Bunyard's Transmission and Parts on my next I-20 trip.

About six months later, I did pay them a visit. This time I was better dressed. I didn't look or smell like a hiker who'd been in the woods for a week. When I pulled up into their shop yard which was behind a house and trailer, I saw a large sign on the garage that read,

Walking into the shop I asked a fellow for James or Al. He nodded toward a pair of feet sticking out from under a Chevrolet. "That's Al. James is gone today."

I knew he didn't recognize me as he stood up. I said, "You don't remember me, do you?" He squinted his eyes in concentration trying to remember my face. I helped him out, "I'm the Louisiana fellow you changed the drive shaft for last year."

A smile of recognition came over Al's face as he said, "Yeah, you're the guy who wrote that book. I liked those stories." We visited a while and I handed him several jars of homemade may haw jelly from home. Leaving, I said, "I'll try to stop in any time I'm in this neck of the woods."

Since then I've been by there several times. Each time I try to bring something as a sign of appreciation for how they helped back in August 2001. They now have two books, a Dry Creek cap, a camp mug, and several other items.

On my last visit at Bunyard's I told Al, "One day I'm going to put you and your dad in one of my books." He grinned as if I was just kidding.

Well, what you're holding in your hands and reading right now is one more promise to the Bunyards that I've tried to keep.

If you happen to be traveling along on I-20 and you near the Alabama/Mississippi line, take the Toomsuba exit and go south about one mile. You'll see it on the right- Bunyard's Transmission and Parts.

They're good people and they'll help you any way they can… Tell them I said "Howdy, and thanks again."

…Just don't try to pay them with an out of town check.
…Or tell them you're a Baptist.
  …And if you've got a fish on the back of your car,
    drive like Jesus would.

"A $1000 Saddle on a $100 Horse"

This story was told to me by my friend Diann Cain Brown several years ago and it is still among my favorites.

Diann's family has always been active in rodeos. Her parents, Junior and Anita Cain made sure their three daughters, Diann, Dena, DeAnn were busy with both horses and basketball.

Junior Cain once told that a neighbor asked him, "Why in the world do you spend so much money on those girls?" His replay was succinct but wise,

"Well, I believe I can pay now or I'll end up paying later." I like his child-rearing philosophy - Keep them busy doing positive things and you can usually avoid paying for it later.

Diann, who taught at our schools for many years, told of returning from a rodeo in east Texas. They stopped at Dairy Queen in DeRidder to get some late night ice cream on their way home.

When they returned to their truck and trailer they quickly saw that one of their saddles had been taken while they were inside. It was a nice expensive saddle that one of the girls had won at a recent rodeo. It was engraved with her name and the date of the reward.

They were disgusted that someone would steal this saddle during the short time they were inside.

They made a theft report to the DeRidder Police Department. As the officer finished his report, the Cain family knew they had probably seen the last of this saddle.

The following Monday Diann received a call from Detective Jimmy Smith. He had a few more questions to ask and finished with, "I tell you what, we'll find your saddle." Diann was more amused than hopeful at Detective Smith's confidence in solving the crime.

However, about two weeks after the theft, Detective Jimmy Smith called again. His first words were, "I've got your saddle, and you can come get it when you're ready."

Diann was thrilled and had to ask, "How in the world did you find it?"

Jimmy Smith chuckled, "We just kept patrolling the area until we saw a $1000 saddle sitting on a $100 horse."

Sometimes I'll see something and Dep. Smith's quote comes back to me. Such as when I see a man giving up his family... for a job... for a short affair, something that will cost him the rest of his life, and it's pretty obvious.

There is no way we should take the precious things in life and put them on something temporal and cheap. The "$1000 saddles" of our lives are the things that really matter. Those "precious things" are not material but people and spiritual possessions; our family, friends and faith.

No man or woman who has a handle on those three areas will be putting the saddle on the wrong horse.

If he or she does, they'll quickly say, "Whoa, I'm on the wrong horse and I'm going the wrong way!"

Another story of "price fixing" occurred many years ago at a Wal-Mart store. This was in the days before 24-hour super centers, bar codes, and exit door alarms.

During the night three burglars slipped in through a skylight into a Wal-Mart. During the several hours they spent inside they did not "take" anything. Instead they spent their time switching price tags on various items. Then as quietly as they came in, the thieves left by climbing out.

Early the next morning among the early-shopping housemaids and last minute fishermen were our three burglars. They each got a shopping cart and went to shopping big time. Soon their buggies were full, crammed

with an assortment of normal-priced items along with some great deals like
- A new VCR for $12.99
- A $2.49 toaster

Being men, they spent lot of time in the automotive section resulting in great deals on batteries, floor jacks, and air compressors. . . and too many more "bargains" to name.

It goes without saying they were caught before they got too far past the store. I can just imagine their quizzical looks as they held up an $8 Skil saw and exclaimed to the security guard, "Well, I thought it was a low price too, but I figured y'all were just having a good sale." I can hear one of them parroting Wal Mart's slogan, "Always low prices!"

It's a humorous story but once again contains a nugget of truth:

We humans are good at "switching price tags." But we'll do it on something far more valuable than a Skil saw. We can easily be guilty of switching the price tags on "things" and those we love.

Because all of us have treasure buried somewhere...Where is yours?

Finally, the article on the Wal-Mart robbers said they had actually switched the price tags. I'd like to have seen the lady who picked up the box of Fruit Loops that were tagged for $62.39.

A big part of our happiness in life is the result of where we put our price tags. What is important is shown by where we place our time, love, energy, and talents.

May it be said of each one of us that we put the right saddle on the right horse... and the right price tag on the things that *really* have value... and *really* matter.

Whip-poor-will Day

You won't find it on any calendar. Most people have never even heard of it. However, it's a day I always think about when it rolls around.

The day is April 6.
It is Whip-poor-will Day.

To understand Whip-poor-will day, you must know a little something about the bird it is named for.

The Whip-poor-will is a member of the Nightjar, or Goatsucker family. This includes its cousins, the Poor-will, and the Chuck-will's Widow, plus the Common Nighthawk, which we call a "bullbat" in the South.

This family of birds is nocturnal and eats insects as they fly. They are gifted with several features that make this possible. First they have large eyes for seeing in the twilight and at night. Then they have a wide mouth for catching insects on the fly. Additionally they possess bristles on each corner of their mouth that acts as fences to keep the insects caught from escaping.

Because whip-poor-wills only become active at night, they are very seldom seen. Because of their "dead leaf" camouflage pattern, they blend in well with the surrounding woods, making them nearly impossible to find in grass or on the forest floor.

Their designation as "goatsuckers" goes back centuries to rural Europe. Peasants, seeing their activity at dusk as they flew around, and even under, herds of goats and cattle, believed they were sucking milk from the animals. In reality, they were zooming in for the insects buzzing around the animals.

During the day, they rest lengthwise on tree limbs or in thick grassy and leaf-covered areas.

In fact, I'm not sure I've ever seen a whip-poor-will. I've seen a darting bird at dusk that was near the call of one, but I'm not positive it was a whip-poor-will.

But I've heard them many times. Their call is from which their name is derived. Their three syllable call says, "whip-poooor-will" with a strong emphasis on the first and last syllable. Bird books describe the call as "purple rib." To attempt to describe this bird's call on paper does not do it justice. Even a recording of its call, as found on a CD of bird calls, is far short of hearing this bird in its natural environment.

The whip-poor-will's sorrowful call must be heard in the woods at twilight or first light it is a soft, touching, and mournful call. Roger Tory Peterson calls it, "a voice in the night."

This mournful solo call is what Hank Williams was talking about in the song, *"I'm So Lonesome I Could Cry."*

Hear that lonesome whip-poor-will,
He sounds too blue to fly.
Like me he's lost the will to live,
I'm so lonesome I could cry...

In many parts of our country, from Arkansas northward, the whip-poor-will's call is a common sound. I once camped alone on the Kiamichi River in Western Oklahoma and was serenaded all night long by a trio of these calling birds. For the first hour I really enjoyed hearing them. After that the thrill of their calling was gone, so I stuffed toilet paper in my ears. (It works - I've used it often when camping with loud snorers.)

I once read about a camper who counted a solo whip-poor-will's call 256 consecutive times at about a steady twenty second interval. The bird's calls, and their corresponding intervals, were perfectly timed for this ninety minute period.

Here is why hearing a whip-poor-will is a noteworthy event in my part of Louisiana: The whip-poor-will does not breed or winter in the southern parts of our state. It passes through Louisiana twice yearly - first on its' journey south to winter in Central America, as far south as Honduras.

On this fall journey the whip-poor-will has no voice. It stays here for a short period until the next cold front moves it on south across the Gulf.

Then on its' return northward flight, it only stays a few weeks in our state. On this spring visit, it is now ready to sing and call. Beginning in late March through the first three weeks of April, whip-poor-wills can be heard calling throughout the wooded areas and fields of our state.

There are times I've heard what seemed to be a nearby call and tried to slowly approach the area and flush this bird, but I've never succeeded.

My dad first informed me about "Whip-poor-will Day." He had been told about it by his grandmother, who had been told about it by her grandmother. Here is what he passed on to me:

"You'll hear the whip-poor-will many evenings at the end of March. As April arrives, more of the birds have arrived from their winter homes. By mid to late April you'll notice that their calling is heard much less until it stops as the first truly hot days return to Southwestern Louisiana."

Dad continued, "But since I was a small boy and was told about April 6 being Whip-poor-will Day, I've never failed to hear one call at dusk on that day. That's why my grandmother and the other old settlers called it 'Whip-poor-will Day.' And I've found it to be true - you'll always hear a whip-poor-will in the edge of Crooked Bayou swamp on this day."

So whenever I can on April 6, sometimes at first daylight, but most of the time at dusk, I return to the Old House and sit on the steps just listening. There have been several times when I was ready to give up and drive home because of the gathering darkness, and then I would finally hear that unmistakable call -

"Whip poooor willll"

Sometimes it would be close to my spot on the front steps. At other times it would be faint and far off in the swamp, but each year I have been rewarded for my journey to hear the whip-poor-will's call on April 6th.

I'll close with my most memorable Whip-poor-will Day. It was in 1991. My maternal grandmother had passed away and my grandfather, Sidney Plott, had come to live with my parents. "Grandpa Sid," as his three grandchildren lovingly called him, was a serious bird watcher. He had had a lifelong interest in birds and their habits for all of his eight decades of life.

We all missed my grandmother, especially her husband of sixty-two years. But I'll cherish those last two years he lived with us in Dry Creek.

The legend of Whip-poor-will Day had come from my dad's side of the family, who had lived in this corner of Beauregard Parish since before the Civil War.

Early that spring, I told Grandpa Sid, about the legend of April 6th and Whip-poor-will Day. Because this story came from the other side of my family, I'm not sure he put much confidence in this legend. He looked at me with twinkling eyes and a slight smile as if he wasn't sure I was kidding or not.

In 1991, April 6th was on a Saturday. As the sun set behind the pines Grandpa and I went out south of my parent's home. As we leaned on an old fence gazing across a cleared area in the dusk, I remember praying that God would be kind and have a whip-poor-will call. I realized that God probably had a lot more going on than worrying about calling whip-poor-wills, but I reminded myself that Jesus said that His Father knew when a sparrow fell, so I figured he cared about whip-poor-wills too.

We hadn't been there very long when a nearby Whippoor-will called. It startled both of us and my grandpa's earlier slight smile turned into a knowing grin.

From far away, we heard the faint return call from another bird deep in the swamp. We just stood there silent, leaning on the fence, each one deep in thought.

I know why my tongue was silent - any attempt to speak would have brought tears. Grandpa stood there quietly with a far off look in his eyes. I wasn't about to interrupt or pry into his heart at this time. To me it was a sacred moment... and many times sacred moments are best spent in silence.

I hope God blesses me with a long life. The length of our lives is in His hands and we must trust Him completely. I'd sure like to be around long enough to one day stand with one of my grandchildren, or even better yet, a great-grandchild, and share this story I'm now sharing with you.

They say that an older person spends lot of time looking back into the past as their life nears an end. I'm pretty sure that is exactly what Grandpa was doing as darkness came on that April day in 1991. I think he knew this was probably his final spring in life, as well as his last Whip-poor-will Day.

And it was...

Two excellent books served as resources on the traits and habits of the whip-poor-will. *A Field Guide to the Birds* (Eastern Edition 4th Edition, copyright 1980) by Roger Tory Peterson is considered the bible of birders.
Additionally, *Louisiana Birds* by George Lowery, tells of birds in their Louisiana habitat. Although out of print, (LSU Press, copyright 1960) this book is available through used bookstores as well as online.

A Song for the Wayfaring Stranger

I had a dream last night… and it was a good one. From a room next door I heard someone singing my favorite song, "The Wayfaring Stranger." The song was sweet, but what was sweeter still was the familiar voice singing it. It was my Dad.

I walked into that room and there was my dad, singing the first song he ever sang in public as a young boy. It was the most requested song that he sang for the rest of his life:

I am a poor wayfaring stranger
Traveling through this world below.
There is no sickness, toil, or danger
In that bright land to which I go.

I'm going there to meet my Father.
I'm going there no more to roam.
I am just going over Jordan.
I am just going over home.

Waking later, I realized that it was only a dream. My dad has now been gone for nearly two years. However, I am still daily thankful for his life. I continue to be amazed at how many lives he and my mom have touched. On the night of his public viewing at the funeral home, people stood in a long line that stretched outside, for over four hours, to pay their respects.

It was both humbling and gratifying to realize that my father, though never rich or famous, had touched so many people of every description.

My oldest son Clay said it best as he spoke at his grandpa (and namesake's) funeral. He held up a framed picture of Daddy crossing the finish line as he won the state championship in the hurdles.

Clay said, "Many people will say that my Papa lost his fight with cancer, but I want to correct that. He did not lose the fight, instead he won a prize. As Paul states in 2 Timothy 4:6, *'I have fought the good fight, I have finished the race, I have kept the faith.'* "

Yes, my dad lived his life investing in *heavenly treasures*, not those that show up in a bank account or a balance sheet....

Dad loved the third verse of "The Wayfaring Stranger" which went:

I want to sing salvation's story,
When I get up there with all my friends,
I want to wear a crown of glory,
I want to touch those nail-pierced hands.

When he sang, "When I get up there with all my friends," he would point out into the audience at his many friends who loved him dearly.

That was always a touching moment for me and I'll cherish that song, and especially that verse, for the rest of my life.

Then he would continue:

I'm going there to see my Savior.
I'm going there no more to roam.
I am just going over Jordan.
I am just going over home.

. . .And that is exactly where I believe my dad is: singing salvation's story. He's singing it to Jesus his Savior, and he's singing it with his friends.

My father wrote the following statement in 1987. Over the years it has given comfort to many people when they have lost a loved one. I hope it speaks to you as it has to others.

Our Father Knows Best

I do not know when or how Jesus will choose to call me home. It may be through something that the world would class as a tragedy or an accident. It might be through a lingering terminal illness, or it might be through the wearing out of this body. It might even be through His coming again. It may be today or many years from now. Regardless, the thing that will make it blessed is that it will be <u>His</u> time and at <u>His</u> call. This will be His call for me to enter the "real" world prepared for me and too glorious to describe.

I do not associate my death with evil in any way, nor do I want my friends and family to view it as such. It is the door through which we all must pass, but the Keeper of the Door has promised that once we make Him Savior and Lord, He will never, never leave us or forsake us. I think this means that neither Satan, nor any power, can ever touch me whether it is in life or at the time of death. Nothing can penetrate the loving arms of Christ around His child.

I believe that God must be either active or passive in the events of life and in this world. In the Bible I only see Him as an active God. I am so glad that He is active in the affairs surrounding my life, and since God never does anything part way, I know He is in control of every second of every hour I live. There is an appalling thought connected with this truth: He has a perfect will for each moment, each day, and each year of my life. . . and I daily fail to even start to live up to this will.

The sweet thing is He still loves me in my weakness just as I will always love my children even when they do different from what I think they should. If I can feel this way about my children in my imperfect love, how much more He can in His perfect unlimited love.

I do not understand why the Lord allows certain things to happen to His people. I do not begin to understand the mind of an all sovereign God. (How could we in our weak and feeble minds?) God does not ask us to figure everything out, but He does ask us to trust Him in every situation and praise His Name because He knows best and will give us what is best.

It is so wonderful just to be able to cling to and claim verses like Psalms 56:3, *"When I am afraid, I will trust in you."* Or Proverbs 3:5-6, which states: *"Trust in the Lord with all of your heart, lean not on your own understanding. In all your ways acknowledge Him, and He shall direct your paths."* Then the verse that says it all, Romans 8:28, *"For all things work together for good to those that love the Lord."* I cling to these verses and find comfort for every thing I cannot understand. God wants us to trust Him and to lean not on our own understanding.

I don't know how the unsaved person can even bear to think about death, much less experience it. I do not know how anyone can make it through life without a guide. I am so glad and so very thankful that I have a Savior who I can trust each moment and who I know will someday call my name when He is ready for me to see Him face to face. My death may be a shock, a surprise, or even called an accident from this side of life's curtain, but to God it will not be a shock or a surprise. It will be a part of God's perfect plan and for me a glorious *Welcome Home*.

Job said it all when he said, *"The Lord gave. The Lord has taken away. Blessed be the Name of the Lord. "*

-Clayton Iles   1987

Signs of the Sign Phantom 1974-1992

Everyone's favorite story from my previous book, *The Old House*, was "The Sign Phantom." It told of my dad's hilarious roadside signs as you entered the community of Dry Creek. The following is a list of all the signs as he remembered them. You may not understand them all. (You would have needed to have been there on some of them.) But they are representative of his neat sense of humor:

>Flag burner - you have been warned!
>Peacocks At Large
>Caution - Adults at Play
>Register for free Ford Torino
>Home of the Bionic Dog
>Airport next exit
>No diving from this bridge
>Toll Bridge - one half mile
>Shop our modern mall

The original Sign Phantom work (circa 1974)

Gateway to Doodle Fork
Going on vacation? - visit Reeves
Famous for Nothing
It sure ain't heaven
We have a great sense of rumor
Stay at our "no-tell" motel
Danger - Skylab landing area
Welcome to Fantasy Island
Get rid of ugly fat - divorce him
One horse town with a sick horse
Equal rights for men rally Saturday
Stop in and make an enemy
Just opened - Tattoo Parlor

Annual Sideburn Pageant
Nude Bathing at Morrow Bridge
Hee Haw filmed here
Now open: Massage Parlor
The Shah will not spend Christmas in Dry Creek
Billy Carter would like Dry Creek
Crossroads to nowhere
Hunters get help - join doe shooters anonymous
Welcome Cuban refugees
Our wives: Maybe, Our guns: Never
Under quarantine: Sleeping sickness
Just happy primitive people here
Move the Olympics to Dry Creek
We ain't gonna give our hogs no flu shots
Satellite capital of the world
Herb lives in Dry Creek *(from the famous Burger King ad)*
Night Hunters - look out for Rudolph
Remember what happened to Grandma
Wedding Saturday night, Baptist Church - Bo and Hope
Our sex symbol: Alan Tumey
(referring to a well known nerdy KPLC-TV reporter)
Deep in the heart of taxes
Protected by Patriot Missiles
"Stormin' Norman" could not control this place
On this site in 1901: Nothing Happened
Yield right-of-way to fire engines
First annual fire ant festival next weekend
Ban all elections*
Shame on you, Edwin*
Come back, Treen*
Gov. Edwards crapped out*
What election?*

* Daddy loved to poke fun at politics and elections, especially anything that involved Edwin Edwards.

We dance with Coyotes
Don't tell us wrestling is fake
J.R. would have a ball around here
Winter home of Bigfoot
Welcome Patty Hearst
Deer Hunters: Bambi – No/Bambi's mother – Never!
Bo don't know Dry Creek
Home of the Ugly Trucks
Killer bees, death awaits you here
River boat gambling on Whiskey Chitto
Come back Charley Mac
Do not shoot squirrels that wave or smile at you
Our deer are armed and trained to shoot back
Waiting for the lottery to make us all rich
Opening here soon - Dr. Red Duke's medical center
Free the 3 gar trapped in Bundick Lake
Welcome to Saturday Night Dead
Boyhood home of Spuds McKenzie
1064 - The combined IQ of everyone in Dry Creek
Entering the time tunnel
Beware of Rabid squirrels
Home of "Black" Iles - tour guide dog
Since we gave up all hope - we feel lots better
Khadaffy wouldn't last 30 minutes here
No bungee jumping off Dry Creek Bridge
Where caterpillars grow on trees - not money
Latest gossip just ahead
2 - Live Crew in concert here Saturday

Do not pet or tease our coyotes
We miss you Boss Hogg
Take a stray dog to lunch
Don't laugh your daughter may marry a Dry Creek boy!

One of the first signs, a favorite of many Dry Creekers.

The Falcon

As you can see, my Daddy had a wonderful sense of humor. You had to know him well to be exposed to how he loved making fun of everything. He could really surprise you at times.

We had an old 1963 Ford Falcon that had been passed around in our family. It had once been blue but by about 1980 it was more rusty primer than blue. It was a small car, good on gas, low on glamour, and had well over 200,000 miles on the odometer. I remember when my parents told my sister, Colleen, she could take it to college for a few weeks. She refused, even though it meant walking and getting rides. She said she didn't want to be seen driving anything that looked that bad.

My youngest sister Claudia shared it with my mom. We razzed little sister about having a car to go to school in when we older siblings once had to ride the bus. But having the Falcon in the high school parking lot meant a lot of good-natured laughter from your peers, so I guess it wasn't too much of a prize; it often lost its brakes, among other things.

Even though the Falcon was ugly, it was a driving machine. It had good acceleration and with the wind blowing in through the open windows, (no AC in the Falcon) you felt as if you were going much faster than you actually were.

I'm not sure when, or why, Daddy decided to sell the Falcon, but he got creative on his ad. In that issue of the Beauregard Daily News he placed this ad:

BEAUREGARD NEWS, DeRidder, La. 70634

FOR SALE: 1963 Falcon. Looks like hell, runs like a spotted ape. $200. Call 328-7362.
2-2chg

My parents said the phone rang off the wall that evening. Daddy sold it quickly to a boy from Singer, which I thought was pretty appropriate. It was a country car and deserved a country owner.

Years later, men still come up, get their wallet out, and hand me a tattered newspaper clipping. Grinning, they will comment, "Do you remember when your dad put this ad in the paper?"

I always assure them I remember it well.

Uncle Quincy's Goose

"He who guards his mouth and his tongue keeps himself from calamity" . -Proverbs 21:23

I'm writing this story while hiking on the Appalachian Trail. This morning I'm sitting in a hiker's shelter on the side of a mountain. It is a mild mid-month May afternoon. The birds have been singing and so is my heart.

Yesterday, I walked all day without seeing one person. I saw chipmunks, spring wildflowers, and great mountain vistas... but no hikers. I heard voices sing all day: turkeys gobbling, the call of hawks, and the sounds of my panting climbing over two mountains... but I never heard a human voice.

Arriving at Deer Park Shelter right before dusk, no one was there. I had it all to myself... I could put my gear down wherever I pleased and do as I wished.

Walking alone all day gave me time to think... Many problems and tough situations began to bubble to the surface of my consciousness. Initially this troubled me... Here I am nearly 800 miles from home and I've brought along my burdens. Walking alone these problems began to untangle themselves and one by one were able to deposit them in their own little worry-proof compartment.

I recalled the Latin saying I have on my desk at work,
"Solivator Ambulando -"
The difficulty is solved by walking.

These difficulties are truly often solved by walking. Tough situations and challenges also seem to shrink down to reality... No longer do they seem mountain-sized but now appear as a simple easily climbed hill.

The quietness, the loneliness, the crisp mountain air, and the grand vistas have all conspired to clear out my mind... I've found that it often takes two to three days to reach this relaxed state.

One of my favorite verses, which I quote often, but sadly do not always live by, comes to mind,

"...Be still and know that I am God..." (Psalms 46:10)

This walking time has surely been a time of fellowship with God... As I've walked, I have thought about quietness, the "friendly loneliness" of spending an extended time alone. After more than a day alone, it is even startling when speaking out loud to yourself.

This gift of human communication is a wonderful thing. But the corresponding trouble this ability to speak gets us in is not very wonderful or good. Walking along, several really funny stories concerning our tongues (and their misuse) come to me.

Solomon in his book of wisdom called Proverbs makes a statement,

"Even a fool is thought wise if he keeps silent."
(Chapter 17:28)

We've all had experiences where we learned the merits of keeping our mouths shut. It is a sad and true fact that words, once uttered, cannot be taken back.

You are probably familiar with the old story of the gossip who was confronted for spreading an untruth throughout the community. The offending "tale-bearer" apologized and volunteered to go back to everyone to whom she had told the lie.

The offended person, who was also very wise, took the gossip out on the front porch and tore open a tattered feather pillow. The wind blew the small downy feathers in every direction. Looking at the gossip, the wise person said, "Trying to track down everyone who has since heard your story is like trying to gather back all of these feathers is impossible."

This "featherweight story" is a good thing for all of us to remember - Once our words are spoken, they are "recorded." The following illustration from my school principal years is a good example:

School administrators hate phone calls from between about 4:00 to 6:00 PM. The chances are it is an unhappy parent who is ready to "raise Cain" about some incident with a teacher, bus driver, or another student.

So arriving home this particular evening, I cringed when I saw that there were several messages on my answering machine.

Sure enough the first message was from an angry parent. A loud voice screamed into the phone:

"Curt, this is Tommy. I want you to know that I'm mad about what happened on Bus 6 today and I'm going to get hold of that bus driver, and when I get through with him, I'm going to come after you. You'd better call the Sheriff's Department to come protect you because..."

You get the drift, don't you? He continued on his tirade and promised to do several things to me that were anatomically impossible.

It made me mad. Tommy, a former classmate from high school, didn't even tell me what the problem was. I sure couldn't quite understand why I needed a butt whipping too.

Angrily, I then made a mistake... I erased the message.

After hearing the next message I knew the two combined recordings could have brought me fame and an appearance on one of those "craziest moments" type of shows.

The second message, left about an hour after the first, was much more subdued. Sure enough it was Tommy again. Clearing his throat nervously, he said,

*"Uh... Curt, this is Tommy again. Well, I found out a little more about what actually happened on the bus. Just, just... uh, **disregard that first message.**"*

I was so hacked off that I erased this message, too! Minutes later I realized that I had lost a jewel in the recordings of Tommy's two calls.

Tommy's calls, especially the first one, are indicative of how we need to think before we talk... because our speech is being "recorded." Maybe not on an answering machine, but just as importantly, by the ears around us. And many times these are little ears that are learning from our words.

Over and over we are confronted about the importance of our words. Once out and "recorded" what we say will bless or curse others, but they cannot be taken back.

We get into trouble when, no matter how well meant, we begin to open our mouths and attempt to impart our knowledge.

I close with what is probably my favorite story on our words and the folly they can create:

My great-great uncle Quincy died before I was born. All that I knew of him came from his niece, my precious Grandma Pearl.

She loved telling stories of her mother's family and their lives in the Cajun community of Oberlin. Mama Pearl had many good stories, but the one she loved telling best was how her Uncle Quincy escaped from Angola Prison by swimming on the back of a mule across the Mississippi River.

Mama's beautiful blue eyes would sparkle as she told of his visit a few nights later to gather some items he needed. She related that he was still dressed in his prison clothes after hopping a series of freight trains and car rides to get back home.

As I became older, it amazed me at how the Godliest person I've ever known - my grandma, could be so proud of her uncle who had escaped from prison. But she loved her family and was always glad to tell the story one more time.

She told this specific story about a goose hunt Uncle Quincy went on. He and two other men were hunting in the rice fields near Oberlin. They had an extremely successful hunt, shooting down many geese.

Laying out their collection of dead geese they were surprised to see that one of the birds had a large metal band on its leg. Closer scrutiny revealed the band had a number and instructions on how to forward this number to the National Wildlife Service.

A further count surprised them that they were one goose over the limit. A quick recount confirmed the fact they had one too many geese to be legal. They were not about to leave a goose behind, so they picked up their geese, tying their legs of the geese together and hoisted them over their shoulders.

Nearing the edge of the field and their vehicle, they decided to leave behind one of the geese at the fence corner. This would mean they would be right on the limit of geese. Their plan was to come back and get the lone goose if they didn't encounter a game warden at their vehicle.

It was a good decision because a federal game warden was waiting for them in the bushes near their vehicle. Together the men laid their geese in a line for counting, placed their guns on the ground for inspection, and took their licenses out of their wallets. Federal game wardens are pretty picky and are not beholden to the local politics that state wardens must endure.

It took a while for the inspections and counting to take place. There just seemed to be need for a little small talk to make the time move quicker, so Uncle Quincy decided to liven up the conversation with this innocent remark, "You know one of those geese we killed had a metal band on its leg."

The federal game warden stood up from his inspection. It was evident he was very interested in Uncle Quincy's statement. He asked, "Really, I'd like to see it and record the number for our study."

(Reader, now I know you are probably getting ahead of me here, but I'm peddling as fast as I can!)

The hunters and the game warden began to look for the goose with the metal band. After several attempts sorting through several dozen geese and finding no leg band, the warden looked up quizzically at Uncle Quincy.

Now, you already know what Uncle Quincy and his hunting buddies knew: the goose with the leg band was "hiding" back in the weeds at the fence corner.

Finally, after the four of them searched through the geese once more, the game warden's stare met Uncle Quincy's eyes. Uncle Quincy couldn't think of but one thing to say,

"Well, I guess it must have fallen off between here and the blind."

With that the game warden snorted disgustedly, abruptly stopped his inspection, and left without saying another word.

After the game warden got out of earshot, Uncle Quincy made a classic statement to his hunting partners,

*"Well, they've never sent a man to the pen
for keeping his mouth shut!"*

I often think of Uncle Quincy's goose when I get in a bind due to excessively running my mouth.

The wise writer of Proverbs said it well, "Where there is abundance of words, sin is not absent."

Even James, the brother of Jesus said it so well, "If anyone considers himself religious and yet does not keep a tight rein on his tongue, he deceives himself and his religion is worthless."

Jesus best summed it up:

"But I tell you that men will have to give account on the Day of Judgment for every careless word they have spoken. For by your words you will be acquitted, and by your words you will be condemned."

-Matthew 12:36-37

It is good to remember that our words are recorded by those around us . . . And most importantly they are both heard, and "recorded" by the very ears of God.

The Proverbs reading plan:

Several times in the story above I have quoted from the wonderful book of Proverbs. It is full of short, wise sayings written especially to inform and educate young men and women.

I'd like to encourage you to read a chapter a day from this book of wisdom. Because of its' length of thirty-one chapters, you can read the chapter that corresponds to the day of the month, reading through the book each month.

A Wade in the River

These next two stories are compiled from recent trips I made to Asia. In 2002 I visited Vietnam and Cambodia. Then last year I went to China. To see another part of the world so different from ours has been both an eye-opening and life-changing experience.

One of the Southeast Asian guidebooks related, "That Asia means **people** - everywhere you go there are vast crowds of people." It is as if a huge river of people flows everywhere - especially in the large cities such as Saigon, Hong Kong, and Phnom Penh. But this river of souls is also swift and deep in the rural areas.

These stories are about what I saw and experienced during my "wade in the river."

The author cools his feet in a Chinese river

Suzie Q

Somewhere in China   October 2003

I'll never see her again on this earth - however I'm certain we will meet in Heaven. I also believe that I'll recognize her when we meet again. I'll know her because of her unforgettable eyes.

We only met her twice and I never even got her name. We really didn't get to visit because she knew no English and I don't speak Chinese. In addition, our meeting was brief because she was in great danger due to the bags she brought to our four man team.

Our only instructions were that she would meet us at the local train station that next morning at 7:45. Because we didn't know her, she would have to find us. There was no way we would ever find her in this river of Chinese faces passing by us. We knew we shouldn't be too difficult to find: four tall and pale Americans with backpacks stand out pretty good in China.

The morning of our meeting was October 1, which is the national holiday for China. For the entire week all businesses and offices close down. Because of this, October 1 is the biggest travel day of the year. The train station was unbelievably crowded. We stood outside in a sea of people - all trying to get through the two doors into the staging area.

We kept looking around. Over and over we would see a young Chinese woman laden with bags and whisper, "Do you think that's her?"

...Finally we saw her coming - her nervousness was a dead giveaway. Following behind her were two porters each shouldering a long bamboo pole with bags on each end. Approaching us, her eyes darted back and forth nervously. This might seem like a game to the four Americans, but to her this meeting was deadly serious. She handed our leader Randy a cell phone programmed for our emergency use. Then she handed him train tickets for our five-hour ride south. Finally, she pointed to the bags and then directed us toward the crowded station entrance.

But before leaving, she looked deeply into our eyes. Her earlier look of nervousness was replaced by eyes showing grim determination and commitment. Those eyes seemed to say, "OK, I've done my part. It's time for you to do yours. It's worth the risk I'm taking to tell others about the difference Jesus Christ has made in my life."

The bags she had brought contained Ziploc bags with DVD's of *The Jesus Film,* plus other tapes and tracts. What made it so special was that the film had been recorded in the heart language of her people. This minority tribe spoke a different dialect from the main Chinese language groups. For the first time they would see and hear the story of Jesus and it would be in their native tongue.

In the coming days as our team hid these packets in woodpiles, under rocks, in the corn and cane fields, and every other place imaginable, I thought often of this brave girl with the bright eyes. She had put herself in great danger to deliver these packages to us.

If we Americans were caught with these materials, we would be unceremoniously escorted out of the country. If this young Chinese woman was caught, the repercussions would be serious - ranging from jail to persecution and difficulties of all types for her, as well as her family.

As Randy, Thad, Ed, and I walked the countryside in the coming days, we talked about this woman. Our brief encounter had left a lasting impression on us. We finally gave her a name, "Suzie Q." From then on that was how we referred to her.

We walked the fields and roads of rural China hiding our precious packets. Our goal was this: We want them found, but hopefully not before we clear out. When we had distributed all of the packets over a period of three days, we once again were instructed by phone to meet Suzie Q, this time at a bus station in a large city.

As our taxi pulled us up to the bus station, there stood Suzie Q beside four more bags containing the gospel. We couldn't help but notice several policemen standing nearby on the sidewalk. The sight of four American strangers picking up four heavy bags after stepping from a taxi had to arouse their curiosity, but no one questioned us. In fact, later one of the friendly policeman inside the terminal directed us to the correct line for our bus.

This time we were going north to another minority people group. These new packets were in a different dialect from our earlier stash. Following us, Suzie walked us into the terminal and ensured we were all right before turning to leave. We never saw her again.

On our way back home we stopped in Hong Kong and met with our contact for this project. We were all curious to find out more about Suzie Q. We were informed that she is a twenty year old Christian. Her livelihood is selling hair combs on the streets of her city. She is very brave and has a deep commitment to follow Jesus, no matter what the cost. She is always ready to perform any service to further the cause of Christ.

Yes, I probably won't see Suzie Q until eternity. When we meet again, she'll find out my name and I'll finally know hers...until then, she'll be "Suzie Q," that brave young Christian with the bright unforgettable eyes...

(The funds for producing the Jesus Film in this language were supplied by the Lottie Moon Mission Offering, a yearly mission's collection among Southern Baptist churches. To learn more about sharing the gospel in China, and how you can be involved, visit www.imb.org.
I highly recommend the ministry of Extreme Missionary Adventures and its leader, Randy Pierce. Their website is www.xmaonline.com.)

Can You Hear Me Now?

A man I encountered in a rural area of Cambodia may have been the defining image of this interesting part of Asia.

I saw him coming before he saw me. He was a rather large man for the Khmer race. What really caught my eye was his attire. All he was wearing was a loose short skirt called a sarong. He was barefooted and bare-chested. Just walking along. I thought to myself, "It's as if we're back in the 19th century here." I quickly wondered if he'd ever seen a television, felt the coolness of air conditioning, or knew how electricity worked.

He did have one modern thing with him. He was smoking a cigarette and blowing the smoke up into the air as he walked along.

He was still a ways from me when I heard a strange noise. It was at the same time familiar as well as unfamiliar. The Cambodian man stopped and reached into his skirt. I quickly saw what it was as he placed it to his ear. He'd just got a call on his cell phone.

He stood there smoking, smiling, and talking as I stared in amazement.

Here was "Mr. 19th century" doing something I can't even do in my hometown- talking on a cell phone! In Dry Creek, Louisiana you're lucky to get two bars showing on your phone. I always tell guests at our camp that they've arrived in the cell phone dead zone. Others call our community the "Bermuda Triangle" of cell phones.

I've told many people of seeing campers at Dry Creek walking the grounds holding their cell phone high in the air, vainly trying to get reception. Once I even saw a man placing his cell phone against our flagpole hoping he'd found a makeshift antenna to connect him to the outside world. (I shouldn't make too much fun because later I went and tried it myself just to see if it made a difference. I can attest it did not.)

Yet here I am 12,000 miles from home. In the middle of a country, Cambodia, where thirty years of civil war and unrest have left a terrible mark and here is a guy using a cell phone. His traditional dress and his embrace of modern technology is an apt description of Southeast Asia, especially Cambodia. A land where the past, present, and future seem to collide together.

Most of all, in Cambodia I saw the open doors of sharing the gospel. The country is a land of young people. Most of the leaders and professionals age fifty and above were killed by the communist Khmer Rouge or escaped the country. There is a great void of leadership and openness to new ideas. Many of the younger generation are disillusioned with the old ways and the traditional Buddhist religion. They are searching and whether they know it or not, the good news of Jesus Christ is what their heart is yearning for.

This is a nation seeking its future and identity. The harvest is ripening. It is worth whatever it takes to be a part of sharing Jesus.

Then I'm reminded of a young American couple I met in Cambodia. They are probably in their late twenties. Both had great careers back in the states. He was a pilot for Delta Airlines. She flew planes for the Air Force. Their future looked bright and limitless.

Their journey to Cambodia started when they came there to adopt a child. Due to widespread disease and violence, there are many many orphans. They did something that so many westerners do when they visit this unusual country - they fell in love with its people. They later returned to adopt another child.

Then they left their secure careers and came to Cambodia. The day I met them, this ex-Delta pilot was helping dig a water well at a village school. He looked happy - just serving the Lord and being part of the harvest.

Over and over I saw examples of talented young people who'd left behind what we call success to serve where the work is hard and the problems are numerous. Working next to them were retired couples who'd refused to buy in to the great American dream of retiring to a condo in South Florida. Instead here they were, signed up for a three year term of serving God half a world away from their children and grandchildren.

I was once again reminded of why missionaries have always been my heroes. Ordinary men and women, with normal problems and faults, who are used by God in an extraordinary way. They've decided to seek the best, while forsaking earthly rewards, while laying up treasures in heaven. It's just a matter of doing whatever it takes to make a difference.

Jim Elliott served as a missionary in Ecuador during the 1950's. His heart was to minister to the unreached Indians of a jungle tribe. After making contact with this tribe and seeming to be making progress, he and his fellow workers were killed by the very people they came to help. Before his death, Elliott made a statement that continues to touch lives today:

"No man is a fool who gives up what he cannot keep, to gain what he cannot lose."

The Cambodian encounter with the cell phone reminds me that technology is a way to reach these seemingly "unreachable" areas. While many types of electronic items have been misused, the spread of the gospel through the internet, DVD's, satellite phones, and computers has been useful in reaching the entire world.

In Acts 1:8, Jesus told His followers, "But you will receive power when the Holy Spirit comes on you; and you will be my witnesses in Jerusalem, and in all Judea and Samaria, and to the ends of the earth."

Going to the "ends of the earth" means getting the gospel out to places that are difficult to reach. Doing whatever it takes, and taking full advantage of every area of modern technology should be part of our strategy to reaching the world.

A Tale of Two Caps

Eight years as a high school assistant principal come in handy at summer camp. At school I handled problems and discipline. The students I spent most of my time with weren't the ones with high GPA's, but rather those who came to see me because of problems, usually of the disciplinary type.

I am amazed now when I see one of those "troublemakers" in Wal-Mart or at a ballgame and they introduce their wife and children. So often they tell of how God has worked in their life since those days when they were getting sent to the office weekly by Mr. Caraway.

From dealing with discipline and roaming the hallways of a school, I developed a sense of "smelling trouble" just by walking past a group of teens. You can often sense that tempers are hot and trouble is brewing. Most of the time, if you can walk the potential combatants away from the crowd, most fights can be averted.

Most actual fistfights result from peer pressure and the need to not lose face in front of your peers. Many times I've come up on a shoving match and stopped it. Most of the time, I could sense that these "would be fighters" were glad to see me arrive to stop the action from going on. By stopping the theatrics and taking them to the office, I was giving them a way to save face (and possibly avoid getting a tail-whipping from the other guy.)

It is also a fact that if two fighters "cool down" in the principal's office, they'll come to their senses and work out whatever caused the problem. Many times I've left two boys in the middle of hotly discussing their reason for the fight. Slipping out I would tell them, "Guys, excuse me but I need to check on something." Closing the door behind me, I would pass by every few minutes and put my ear to the door. Never in my years as a principal did the boys ever break out fighting in my office.

Invariably when I returned they would tell me, "We've worked it out" and their subsequent actions would prove this is exactly what they'd done while sitting in my office. However, I never did this with girls. They are a whole different animal when it comes to fighting and making up.

Always the key to a fight, both in the lead up and action in the day after the fight was other students. There are always students we called "tale bearers." Many times this student would report back and forth between the two angry students, as in "Do you know what John just said about you?"

Once two girls at East Beauregard got into a bad fight by the lockers. This was a hair pulling, scratching, screaming fight that drew a large crowd of spectators. When a teacher brought these two girls in I was extremely surprised. These were two seniors who were normally no trouble at all. It didn't take me long to realize what had precipitated their fight - It was another senior named Mickey.

Now, Mickey was good friends with both girls. But he had taken on the unassigned role of "pony express rider" in passing insults back and forth between the girls.

It was with hidden pleasure that I called Mickey to the office. He entered my office with the classic student statement, "Now what did I do?" I quickly answered his question, "You are the reason those two girls got into a fight." All manner of denials, explanations, and excuses came forth from Mickey. He had a hurt look of righteous indignation that I would even accuse him of starting this fight. It was difficult not to smile as Mickey passionately defended himself. He was everyone's favorite including mine, and always fun to be around.

But he sure didn't like me when I stopped his plea bargaining with this statement: "Mickey, the girls are getting one day of in-school suspension. But that is not what I'm giving you - you're getting two days there for instigating the fight." With a look of horror on his face, he sank back in his chair and exclaimed, "You can't do that to me!!!"

I glanced up from the written discipline form and replied, still with somewhat of a smile, "Well, I just did it."

Even now, fifteen years later I still laugh with Mickey about this incident.

Now this "school fighting resume" is told to illustrate this: *a disciplinarian, even at church camp, can often smell trouble brewing.* That was the case on a recent night of summer youth camp.

The evening service had just ended and campers roamed the area around the snack shack and main road. There was a large group of about twenty-five campers near the road. I could tell something was up. Tension could be felt just walking past this group.

I walked over and tried to say politely, "Hey guys, what's going on here?" The crowd parted slightly but no one was willing to tell me anything. Then I saw Randall and figured he was the person everyone was gathered around.

I've always liked Randall. I had gotten to know him better the previous summer when we made a late night emergency room visit.

Randall is what I call a "man-child." Although only fourteen at the time, he was a big boy-- about six-foot-two and a good 250 pounds. He had the look and size of a high school football lineman. I pulled him to the side and said, "Now Randall, I know something is going on. Tell me what the trouble is." He hesitated but finally began,

"Brother Curt, I've had trouble with some of those boys in cabin 7 and they won't leave me alone."

Looking at Randall and then thinking of what groups were in cabin 7, I knew what the trouble was probably about. Randall was wearing a cap with the Confederate flag on it. One of our groups in cabin 7 was an inner city youth group from the Alexandria area. This group, which had had a great time this week, was composed entirely of black teens.

I turned to Randall and said, "Hey, let's go over here where we can talk." I told him to take off his cap and put it in his pocket. "Randall, does this trouble have anything to do with your cap?" He kind of mumbled a denial but I now knew at least part of the basis of this problem.

I sat him in one of our outdoor pavilions and went over to cabin 7. Outside, the campers were still milling around and talking. I tried to think of how to defuse this situation. That was the exact moment when I spotted the solution to this problem - It was a young man named Ty. He was the oldest and tallest camper from this inner city group. I'd spoken to him several times this week and he had responded with a quiet nod and a shy smile. I just had a feeling that he could help solve this problem.

I walked over and spoke to the guys. Then I called Ty over and asked him if he could help me. He was nice looking and athletic. I had watched him on the basketball court and he could sure play. Ty looked at me suspiciously as we walked away. I told him that we had a problem that I could use his help on. He cautiously said that he would try, but still seemed non-committal about getting involved.

Ty was also wearing a type of cap, but it sure wasn't a rebel cap. It was a thin black nylon stocking cap that many black teens wear.

Bringing these two guys together under the pavilion, I looked at both boys and their caps - Ty's black cap on his head and Randall's confederate cap sticking out of his back pocket. There was a wide chasm that these two caps represented and I knew my work was cut out for me.

We sat down in the pavilion and I introduced the boys to each other by name. They had probably spent most of this day glaring at each other. Now they were no longer nameless but instead were sitting by each other in the darkness on an old church pew. I asked them about their problem but neither guy was willing to say much.

I turned to Ty and asked, "Ty, does Randall's hat bother you?" After a brief silence, his reply was slow and measured, "Well it doesn't bother me too much, but there are some of the guys in our group that are pretty hot and upset by him wearing it."

I asked Randall if he knew why this rebel flag cap bothered these guys from Alexandria. He kind of hemmed and hawed before shrugging, "Well, I just don't think it ought to bother those guys." I shared with him how the same flag that meant freedom and Southern pride to him meant something completely different to a black man. To them it was a symbol of slavery, oppression, and prejudice.

With that I switched on my flashlight and turned to I Corinthians 8. In this passage the Apostle Paul addressed the problem in Corinth of eating meat that had been sacrificed to idols. Paul clearly stated that the actual eating of the meat was in no ways a sin, but he added a passage of wisdom that is still a good rule of thumb two millenniums later. In verse thirteen, he states,

"Therefore if what I eat causes my brother to fall into sin, I will never eat meat again, so that I will not cause him to fall."

Two chapters later Paul adds,

"So whether you eat or drink or whatever you do, do it all for the glory of God. Do not cause anyone to stumble, whether Jews, Greeks, or the church of God."

I turned to Randall and asked, "Do you see any correlation between your rebel hat and this passage in

Corinthians?" Reluctantly he agreed with Paul's wisdom on not being a stumbling block with our actions.

I told Randall of what God had done in my life on this same issue. I am a true son of the South. My great great great grandfather, the first in our line to settle in Dry Creek, joined the Confederate army and later died near Opelousas. All of my life I'd proudly displayed the stars and bars. Then about ten years ago this changed when the realization came that this same flag, which I took such pride in, offended my black friends.

Sitting there in the dark with these two boys, I told how it took several years to make this decision: I had made a personal pledge not to display the rebel flag out of respect for others who might be offended. *No flag or symbol is more important than people.*

I shared with these boys a story I read while visiting Appomattox Courthouse in central Virginia. This crossroads village is where the Civil War ended. Being a lover of history, it was a great day to visit there and walk into the room where Generals Lee and Grant sat down to end our country's bloody four year war.

The story I read was beneath a torn and tattered rebel battle flag. The day after the signing of the surrender, the Southern soldiers were under orders by General Lee to march in, stack and surrender their weapons as well as turn in all battle flags and regimental colors.

On this spring day in 1865, thousands of Union soldiers lined the picket fences along the narrow road through this village. General Grant had sternly ordered that nothing detrimental or disrespectful be spoken toward the defeated Rebels. Standing there at this museum in front of the framed Confederate flag, I could look out the museum window and see the long curving road where these men had marched on that fateful day.

The story in the museum told of how the Southern soldiers quietly stacked their weapons as the Union soldiers stood silently at attention.

As the regimental colors and battle flags were folded and placed on top of the rifles, Southern men wept openly. One soldier lovingly patted the flag and stepped away. As tears flowed down his gunpowder-stained face, he turned toward the Union soldiers and pointed to a United States flag blowing in the wind. Commenting to men of both armies within earshot he said,

> "Men, you see that flag there. That's my flag now. Yes, sir—that's my flag again."

I'm not sure Randall fully appreciated my sermon/lecture/history lesson, but he did nod his head several times in assent. Then I asked Randall, "I'd appreciate you not wearing that cap again at Dry Creek Camp. I'd like to take it and keep it for you until the end of the week."

Randall sat quietly for a few moments and said, "If you'll let me keep it, I promise it will not be seen or worn again." I told him that he needed to promise that to Ty, not me. He reached out his big hand and promised as he shook Ty's hand.

However, Randall wasn't quite through. He turned to me and added as he pointed directly at Ty, "There is one thing about those guys that bothers me."

Had I been closer I would have kicked Randall in the shin as hard as I could. He continued, "It bothers us that we can't wear our hats in the Tabernacle, but these guys can wear their black nylon caps."

I turned to Ty who was listening intently. I asked him, "Ty, Randall has a good point. Could you take care of that for me?" Ty quickly answered, "That is no problem at all. I'll take care of it."

With that we stood and each boy stood in a circle as I prayed for them and all our campers.

I share the tale of the two caps not to make a political or racial statement, but to remind myself that no flag, symbol, or statement, is more important than the feelings of another person.

If I'm living right and have the right attitude, I'll be careful not to insist on my own rights but think about the other fellow.

Randall and Ty both had a good week for the rest of camp. The two caps were not seen again. The heat from this situation was cooled simply by two young men looking into each other's eyes, shaking hands, and having a willingness to look out for someone else's best interests.

May the same be said of all of us…

The Heavenly Choir

It is the Christmas season—The Dry Creek Church choir sings in a beautiful way that cannot be adequately described on any printed page. Today is one of my favorite events of the year- the church Christmas musical. It's much more than just a musical... it's a production... replete with drama, stories, and best of all, inspiring music.

... And as usual it bears the stamp of my best friend, Joe Aguillard. Joe is our music director but he is so much more to our church family. He is the person everyone in our church deeply respects, considers a friend, and who leads us in worship weekly.

For nearly thirty years, since we first met in a biology lab class at Louisiana College, he has been my best friend. As in any long term friendship, we've had countless opportunities to stand beside each other in the joys of raising our families, our years together in education, and in serving the Lord together.

We've also been together in the troubles, trials, and tough circumstances of life that come to us all. Joe is that special kind of friend on whom you can always depend. We share the type of lifetime friendship that is truly, truly priceless.

I'm reminded of a story concerning the Union Generals U.S. Grant and William Sherman. From their earliest days of the Civil War, they worked together and were close friends. Together they shared both triumph and tragedy. Grant, the better known of the two, was once asked, "Tell me about you and General Sherman?" Grant, who was leading the Union Army to eventual victory at this point, replied, "Well, we've both been through some tough times. When he was crazy, he leaned on me and when I was a drunk, I leaned on him. Right now I just believe we're leaning on each other."

Now, my friend Joe has never been a drunk although I've probably been a little crazy a few times, but I do understand Grant's comment on leaning on a special friend in times of need.

As our entire choir sings, I'm reminded of this special friendship I share with our music director.

While the choir sings of the coming of the infant Jesus, a robed couple enters the back of our sanctuary where I'm sitting. It is Tom and Konnie Humphreys. Tom is holding their infant daughter. They are portraying Joseph and Mary. Their youngest daughter, Elizabeth, is baby Jesus.

Tom touches me on the shoulder and movingly says, "Brother Curt, I want you to see my baby son, Jesus." Tom, with his long hair and beard, always looks the part of how I picture Jesus. He is a tall broad-shouldered man with kind eyes.

Tom's introduction of his "son Jesus" is full of emotion, pride, and conviction. It's as if we are sitting back in the first century Jerusalem temple on baby Jesus' first visit there.

What happens next is what makes this moment memorable. Tom moves on through the crowd toward the front. He stops at the seat of Uncle Rob McCracken, the oldest man in our church at nearly ninety. Tom excitedly puts baby Jesus in front of Uncle Rob and his wife, Aunt Iola, and intones, "Uncle Rob, aren't you proud of my son Jesus?" Uncle Rob touches the baby and sweetly strokes her hair. People all over the auditorium are craning their necks and watching.

It is an emotional scene. It's as if Simeon is at last touching the long awaited Messiah he had waited to see and bless before he died.

Tom and Konnie, or rather Joseph and Mary, make their way to the front as the song continues. Tears fill my eyes. I'm once again reminded how music can move our soul like nothing else. It is such a wonderful and precious gift from God.

Then for some strange reason, I think about Carl Mosley and how he loved to sing. Why in the world at this exact moment his name comes to me is one of those mysteries of life.

But I believe my sudden remembrance of Carl is linked to the major reason why I believe God has so generously blessed our church's music ministry.

Carl's story goes back as far as I can remember. He and his family were some of the first people I remember when we moved to Dry Creek in 1960. In our old white church, which sat on the camp grounds across the street from Foreman's Grocery, things were much different than today. I can still see the three old church pews that served as the choir area. There were never a great many folks in the choir, but I always remember Carl Mosley being there among them.

When Joe Aguillard became our music director in the early 1980's, our church had moved up Highway 394 to its present location. Joe inherited a good group of singers, but nothing in comparison to the gifted singers, accompanists, and musicians we now have.

...But Joe also inherited Carl Mosley in the choir. I do not mean it unkindly, but Carl was by far the worst singer I'd ever heard. That statement stands as true today as it did then. I intend no meanness when I state this - Just ask anyone who heard our choir during these years and they'll agree. Carl had a dull monotone voice that was so off key it could always be heard above all the other singers.

Regardless of that, Carl loved to sing. It was very evident that he sang from his heart. I am confident that

Carl's singing sounded "perfect to God's perfect ears." But to all of those listening Sunday after Sunday, his bland monotone singing was making "a joyful noise," but it was more noise than note by note singing.

When the choir did a special, you could always pick out Glenda Hagan's high soprano, Judy Aguillard's beautiful alto, my dad and Donnie Reeves with their enthusiastic bass voices. The words of the singers mixed with the piano playing of Nell Christopher. All these voices and the piano blended together in a beautiful way ... but always hovering just above the harmony was the indescribable sound of Carl's toneless voice.

Joe would sometimes play me the taped recordings of a recent choir special. He'd grimace and say, "Listen, you can hear Carl above everyone else." Sure enough, you could pick him out. His singing always stuck out. I firmly believe if you'd put him in the 600 voice Mormon Tabernacle Choir, a careful listener could still have picked out Carl's singing.

The Mosley family was one of Dry Creek's most interesting families. Mr. Mosley, a big kindly man, had been in World War I and served as a Texas Ranger during the rough years of the early 20th century.

When they moved to Dry Creek the Mosley family lived in an old barn and carved out a living from their land. They were a hard-working family and no one worked harder than the two younger sons still at home, Carl and his brother John

I once visited their home when they were taking eight foot post oak logs, skinning the bark off them, and dipping them in vats of creosote to seal them. The fact that you could easily buy fence posts at numerous places in DeRidder did not stop them from living off their own land.

During the Cold War years when nuclear devastation seemed a real possibility, I would think of the Mosleys. If anyone could survive the aftermath of widespread nuclear war and the resultant breakdown of civilization and famine, they could. They would have just continued living off the land as they'd always done.

Carl was slightly retarded. He could not read and his speech was sometimes hard to understand. However, he could take apart any engine and quickly put it back together in working order. He and John supplemented the family income by cutting firewood and doing chores for people. It was something to watch their wood cutting skills; even in their forties they could outwork men half their age.

Now, Carl could sure cut firewood, but he couldn't sing very well at all...

Carl (left) and John Mosley

Being the 'song-less' son of a well-known singer, I know all about expectations and a little something about music. I've always been what is called a "funeral singer." When a full choir is needed for a week day funeral, I'm happy to supply a warm body and a poor voice. I remember DeDe telling me that if you ever forget your words or get off key, just keep mouthing over and over, "Watermelon, watermelon, watermelon."

In the old days at church, I would always look on as the choir assembled in the loft area. I would watch with a quiet smile as what I called, "Choir basket turnover" occurred. The very good male singers would tactfully try to put a few bodies between themselves and Carl. To stand by him and sing was tough. For some reason no matter how a person's voice was, it tended to gravitate toward Carl's level and tone (or lack thereof.) Even the altos in the middle row tried to get where they were not in front of Carl.

During my infrequent excursions to the choir, I made it a point of standing by Carl. First of all, I sincerely enjoyed visiting with him. But most importantly I knew that I was shielding Ed King, Ken Farmer, or one of the other good singers from Carl's one note song. My "sacrifice" was the musical equivalent of the baseball term of "taking one for the team."

Here is what I love about Dry Creek Baptist Church and my best friend Joe: There was never a word said about excluding Carl Mosley from the choir. His faithfulness and kind spirit was appreciated and his singing was tolerated. I do know that there were times when people made suggestions or comments about removing Carl, especially during special musicals or cantatas.

However no comments ever made it past the person who led that same choir - Joe Aguillard.

Joe was, and is, a tremendous musician and leader. He wants everything to be done with quality and excellence. However, what I love best about my best friend Joe is his heart of kindness and compassion. To *help* the choir and music by *hurting* Carl Mosley was not an option.

Sometimes as the choir would sing and Carl rocked back and forth as he sang, I'd recall the Andy Griffith episode where they tried to exclude Barney Fife from the choir because of his poor singing. They plotted and planned every way possible to keep Barney away. But Mayberry's strategy was never an option at Dry Creek Baptist Church.

In 1990 Carl died suddenly of a heart attack at the age of 52. It was a shock to everyone, especially to our church where the Mosleys were such faithful members. Within a short period of less than two years after Carl's death, both his younger brother John and their mother Lucille also died.

Suddenly the long association of the Mosley family with our church ended. These were members who *never missed* church and they were *greatly missed.* They were faithful and there are few traits better than faithfulness. Their whole life revolved around two things - working hard with their hands and going to church. Once their entire family was recognized for not missing Sunday School for ten consecutive years.

But now their pew was empty... and Carl's spot in the choir was vacant. And regardless of whether the choir sounded better or not, we were all poorer for losing this special family of dedicated Christians.

Returning once again to today's Christmas musical, I scan the large crowd that has filled our nice new sanctuary. I realize that probably not one quarter of those present today would even recognize the names of Curtis, Lucille, John, or Carl Mosley.

But whether our present choir knows it or not, every person singing in this choir, and all of us enjoying it, is connected to Carl... and Joe Aguillard's early years as choir director at Dry Creek. Here is where I'm coming from:

Experience has taught me that many times God will give us *small tests* before He chooses to send us *major blessings*. It is as if He wisely says, "I'd like to give him this wonderful thing, but I'd better make sure he can handle it first." I call these tests "matters of the heart." It is the time when we must choose between what the world would do and what we know deep down in our heart is the right thing to do. I've noticed that these tests most often involve either our dealings with people or material possessions.

Jesus talked about this in several parables, especially in the story of the talents. We are all familiar with His oft-quoted words in Matthew 25:21:

"Well done, good and faithful servant! You have been faithful with a few things; I will put you in charge of many things."

I firmly believe Carl Mosley (and his singing) was just such a test from God. It was a test to our church… and it was a specific test to our gifted music leader.

What was most important… a "perfect choir" or heartfelt singing from a simple man who could have easily been brushed aside? It was this test that was passed with "flying colors" by our church, our choir, and my best friend Joe.

Sitting today in my comfortable seat I look at the stage/choir area. The choir is packed and sings with both musical skill and passion. The voices are blended with piano, organ, keyboard, harp, and guitar. As Tom, Konnie, and their baby stand up front, the choir sings about our Savior Jesus. All throughout the audience both men and women dab their eyes. Even in the choir, members sing as tears flow freely down their cheeks. These emotional expressions only make their singing more joyful and meaningful.

Silently, I thank God once again for the gift of music - for how it allows us to come into His presence for communion, fellowship, and worship through this medium of song. And I know this priceless moment in our church is a result of a once young (sorry, Joe) music leader, who listened with his heart and not just his musical ear.

As we age we naturally think more about Heaven. It's because a lot more of the people we cherish are on that side of eternity. Wouldn't it be nice to know more about what being in God's presence is like. I'm sure it would change the way we all look at this life, as well as how we grieve over death.

I do know that most Biblical references to Heaven include singing and praise. I recall the generations of my family, all with a love for both music and God, and realize they are just getting warmed up for an eternal choir special.

Carl is in that choir. He is there not because he was a good man, although he was just that. Nor is he in God's presence because he probably didn't miss church five times in his adult life. He is there because in his simple child-like mind he came to Jesus seeking forgiveness and new life. There are a lot of things Carl did not understand, but he had a clear view of God, and His son Jesus as the way to Heaven.

In that heavenly choir, Carl Mosley's voice and key is perfect. He sings there with the same passion he sang with here. In the very presence of God he lifts up his voice in perfect harmony...
      In perfect tune...
          In perfect communion with God.

Blessed be the name of the Lord....

Mr. Smith's Plane

On the day of Mr. Smith's plane crash, I didn't hear him fly over Dry Creek.

However, I've thought about him and how his plane crashed into the creek I love, Bundick Creek. I went to the crash site later and there wasn't a limb broken on either creek bank. Evidently the plane had plummeted straight down.

Additionally I guess I've thought about it because the crash site is so close to where the front page picture of my first book, *Stories from the Creekbank*, was taken.

Terry, Curt, and Clint Iles at Bundick Creek, 1999

Then maybe the reason I remember him is because he is a symbol to me, and always will be, of living life to the fullest... right to the very end.

I never met Jim Smith of Austin, Texas. He was seventy three years old on the December 2000 day when his plane crashed into Bundick Creek, ending his life. But I strongly believe I would have liked him. Any man, who at an age when others are whiling away their lives in a rocker, would still be building and flying an airplane is my kind of man.

On that foggy morning when he left out of Georgetown, Texas he was bound for Gainesville, Florida to the home office of the builder of his plane, Team Tango. The purpose of this trip was to put on wheel covers for the plane he had earlier built from a kit.

We'll never know what exactly happened in the cockpit of Mr. Smith's plane. But I'm pretty confident about the first hours of his flight. I can see him whistling, fiddling with the knobs, and enjoying the thrill of flying a plane solo over the woods, rivers, and fields of Texas and western Louisiana.

Flying – it's something that stirs the soul.

As a boy there was an old RCA Victrola phonograph at the Old House. It was played by winding up the handle on the side. It played scratchy records and there was one old weather-beaten record I would always search through the tattered albums to find. It was a song about Charles Lindbergh.

It would start with the faraway sound of a plane engine accompanied by the moaning wind. In my mind I could see Lindy far over the Atlantic Ocean searching for any sign of the Irish Coast. These are the lyrics I recall:

> *Lindbergh, oh what a flying fool was he.*
> *Lindbergh, your name will live in history.*
> *Over the oceans he flew all alone,*
> *Daring to face danger, he flew on his own.*
>
> *Others will make that trip across the sea*
> *Upon some future day...*
> *But take your hats off to lucky, lucky Lindbergh,*
> *The eagle of the USA.*

That urge to fly... to see, go, explore..... Lindy had it, and so did Mr. Smith. You see, it is all about living until you die. Enjoying what you do and doing what you enjoy.

It was ironic that Mr. Smith, who never visited Dry Creek but ended his life here, died just weeks after the death of Mr. Jay Miller, a man who lived in Dry Creek for all of his life. It was evident they shared something in common - a zest to live life fully and to the very end.

Mr. Jay was the last of the eight Dry Creek Miller brothers. He was eighty-three years old when he died. On the day of his death he had started early on a deer hunt. He put his daughter Juanita and his pastor, Glen Ducharme, each on a stand, then hurried on toward his own deer stand. On the way there he fell dead.

Since the day of that last hunt, many men have commented, "Boy, I hope I can go out just like Mr. Jay. He was doing what he enjoyed and still able to do it.

Thinking of Mr. Smith and his last flight as well as Mr. Jay's final hunt, another last hunt story comes to mind.

My Uncle Lawrence told the story of an old hunter in Catahoula Parish. One evening the elderly man went out to his favorite slough to wade up on some wood ducks. When he did not come home after dark, a search was started. When they found him the next morning, he was slumped over dead against a stump in about knee deep water. He was still carefully cradling his shotgun. In one hand he clutched two wood duck drakes. Once again, a man doing what he enjoyed, and being able to do it to the end.

No discussion of older folks living life to the fullest is complete without my friend and hiking partner, Macon "Mac" Rathburn. He is a tough old retired military man who hiked the Appalachian Trail twice during his sixties. In 1996, he took me to hike the northern end of this trail. This last section is known as the 100 mile wilderness and has very few roads and food supply points. At the end of this stretch is the Holy Grail of all hikers - Maine's Mount Katadhin.

It is, as I found out, a tough, strenuous, and unforgiving climb. Ascending Katadhin on a cool August morning, we met several discouraged hikers heading back down, each shaking their head and commenting about the difficulties above tree line.

Eventually we climbed up into the treeless rocky portion of the trail. It was tough climbing and I marveled at Mr. Rathburn, in his seventies, and his gritty determination to summit this mountain one more time.

Climbing up we were met by a trail guide, kind of like a park ranger. He looked at Mr. Rathburn and commented, "Sir, I'd be very careful up here. Two days ago a man about your same age fell, broke his neck, and died up ahead of here."

Mac Rathburn gazed up the climbing rocky path, spat a big brown stream of Red Man tobacco on the ground, and said matter of factly,

"Well, I can't think of a better place
to die than on Katadhin..."

Macon "Mac" Rathburn

"Mac" on Maine's Mt. Katadhin 1996

With that, he hit his walking stick against a rock, and stepped upward and onward...

Once again, here was a man living his life fully and to the end. Not afraid to take a risk... Mr. Smith, Mr. Jay, and Mac had it... I want to have it too.

I thought back to Mr. Smith's plane crash in Dry Creek last year when we learned the terrible news about the loss of the space shuttle Columbia. Everyone has at one time wondered how it would feel to travel in space... to look down on the earth.... to fly at speeds unbelievable even sixty years ago.

How tragic was the death of our astronauts. I've prayed for their families, friends, and co-workers. But once again, I hear the voice of Jim Smith whispering, "Doing what you enjoy. It's worth the risks. Doing what you enjoy... really living..."

Yes, the death of any person is a great tragedy to family and friends. Even when expecting the death of an older sick person, it is still a shock that they are gone.

But to see an older person choose to live life to the last drop, before their time is up, is not a tragedy. It is an inspiration.

John Piper is a great speaker and writer about living life with a passion. In his book, *Don't Waste Your Life*, Piper encourages young people to make bold decisions about what you give your life to. He quotes from a February 1998 *Readers Digest* article and then adds his comments:

"A couple took early retirement from their jobs in the Northeast five years ago when he was 59 and she was 51. Now they live in Punta Gorda, Florida where they go cruising on their 30-foot trawler, play softball and collect seashells."

Piper then adds, "At first, when I read it I thought it might be a joke. A spoof on the American dream. But it wasn't. Tragically, this was the dream: Come to the end of your life - your one and only precious God-given life - and let the last great work of your life, before giving an account to your Creator, be this: "Look, Lord. See my sea shells." That is a tragedy! And people today are spending billions of dollars to persuade you to embrace that tragic dream. Over against that, I put my protest: Don't buy it. Don't waste your life."

John Piper pleads the case for a life invested in the only thing that matters—bringing glory to our Savior and Lord.

Yes, I never met Mr. Jim Smith of Austin, Texas. I do not know anything about his life other than that he was retired from both the military and school teaching. I've tried since the crash to locate his family with no success.

What would I do if I found them? I'd love to spend an evening just hearing about the life of their dad, husband, or friend. A man who evidently lived life to the fullest, even to the end.

With all respect I would share with them my sympathy in the loss of Mr. Smith. If they wanted, I would take them deep down into Bundick swamp and show them where their loved one's plane crashed.

But I don't believe I would tell them that the end of his life was a tragedy. I would hope that they have the comfort of knowing he was doing exactly what he loved best- flying over the woods and rivers, living life with a passion!

The section on John Piper was written by Randy Pierce with Extreme Missionary Adventures. The entire article can be viewed at www.xmaonline.com

Two Reasons Why I Believe in God...

*"How dreadful it would be if we had No One
to thank for all of the glorious things in life."*
                                                -Rosetti

There are hundreds of reasons to believe in a Creator. Writing this story, I think of two recent examples that have grabbed both my attention and interest. It just so happens that both of these illustrations deal with birds.

My sweet wife dislikes Chimney Swifts as much as I love them. This small bird, often called a "chimney sweep" builds its nest in interior places such as hollow trees, caves, and most commonly in the civilized world - in chimneys.

DeDe is not crazy about the noise they make nesting in our chimney each spring. Later as the young begin to leave the nest, they dislodge soot and sometimes a young bird will even fall down into our fireplace and flap about the house.

The Chimney Swift is an amazing bird. First of all, it is unique in that the shafts of its tail feathers are longer than the feathered "webs." These long spines allow the birds to cling vertically to the side of chimneys.

"Sweeps," which are commonly described as "a cigar with wings," feed on the wing. They devour insects as they dart about making a loud twittering sound while flying. They even break off twigs for their nests while in flight. Their fragile nests are built of sticks held together by the secretions of their salivary glands.

Dr. George Lowery in his classic book, *"Louisiana Birds"*, tells several amazing stories on this species: "One of the birds banded at Baton Rouge on September 24, 1938, presumably went to South America to spend the winter. It must have come back through the United States in 1939, for it was captured and released at Campbelltown, New Brunswick, on June 11, 1939. It then presumably went back to South America in the fall, possibly passing through Baton Rouge as it did in 1938. Finally, on August 22, 1940, it was found dead at Upsalquitch, New Brunswick, fifteen miles from the point of its earlier capture and release in 1939."

A look at any world map and an examination of the distance between South America and the Canadian province of New Brunswick, gives a new meaning to the term "frequent flyer."

Dr. Lowery also relates another story of the Chimney Swift's prowess in migration: "Aluminum leg bands that had been placed on 13 Swifts in Tennessee, Alabama, Georgia, Illinois, Connecticut, and Ontario were obtained by a missionary from natives living among the Rio Yanayaco, one of the headwaters of the Amazon in Eastern Peru."

It was unclear as to how long it had taken the tribesmen to examine and collect these thirteen bands. Dr. Lowery said that about one in every 400 swifts caught by birders have a leg band. This meant that the Peruvian tribesmen had possibly caught over 5000 swifts to collect the 13 bands.

I'd like to know what they believed about these bright silver leg bands with strange engravings on them!

Now back to our Dry Creek home and the annual spring visit of our resident Chimney Swifts - As the young are hatched and become feathered the noise from inside the chimney can be bothersome. Soon however, the young birds leave the nest, cling to the sooty chimney wall, and follow the adult birds toward the light and their first flight.

But sometimes a young bird, whether by falling out of the nest or not quite being strong enough to make the upward climb, will fall to the bottom of our fireplace. We don't have a covering over our fireplace, they can really make a mess before you discover their presence in the house.

But to me it is worth the mess to be able to catch one. Usually, I'll use my hat as a scoop and carefully trap the small bird. Grasping the tiny bird with its heart pounding, I've now got soot all over my hands. I walk out through our sun porch into the backyard. With one quick motion I toss the bird from my hat into the sky. Instantly, it takes wing and flies away. Even on its maiden flight it shows the darting noisy flying style so unique to its breed.

Staring in wonder as it disappears across the nearby field I say out loud, "How could anyone watch a bird's first flight and not believe in God?"

Then there is a second reason why I believe in God, and once again it has to do with the bird kingdom.

I see these two birds most afternoons. It seems they are waiting for DeDe when we arrive to walk at the East Beauregard track. We walk and talk away two to three miles as we make our dutiful laps around the oval track.

And my "friends" are always waiting for me on the south end of the track. They are two killdeers. As we walk by their end, our game begins.

The killdeer is a bird easily recognized by its call, "kill- deah," which it repeats over and over, especially when alarmed. A member of the Plover family, which mainly consists of shore birds, it lives and nests in areas throughout Louisiana.

When alarmed, the Killdeer prefers to run rather than fly. They are found anywhere where flat open ground is common.

Its nest is simply a small cavity in the ground. Four small eggs, which are usually speckled with chocolate brown, are laid and guarded by the pair of birds.

When the young are hatched, they very quickly begin running about within minutes.

My two killdeer friends at the track have a nest somewhere in the vicinity of the south end zone. This is evident due to their actions as we approach on each lap.

One of the birds, and sometimes both, will run about near us. Then the game begins: One of the birds will fall pitifully on the grass with a wing stuck out at an unnatural angle. The "broken wing" will quiver as the parent bird, peeping miserably, seems on the edge of death.

My part of the game is to suddenly walk toward the "dying bird." Then it will rise up and limp away, still crippled, leading me on... and away from the hidden nest.

No matter how many laps we walk, they will be waiting each lap to reenact their show. DeDe says they look forward to seeing me each afternoon. She claims they don't do it when I'm not with her.

So I happily play my part in the drama. As the predator, I chase after the parent bird, who is very willing to lead me away from her nest, or from her small hatchling young.

Both the male and female killdeer are identical in pattern - a long-legged bird with two unmistakable black breast bands. Because of that I'm never sure which of my friends are father or mother.

I'd like to think the second Killdeer is the male bird. This is due to his "macho show." As I approach, he will turn toward me and slowly advance. While doing this, he will puff up his body by spreading his wings and fluffing his tail feathers.

Believing bigger is better, he presents this bigger silhouette as he advances on these tall intruders of his nesting area.

If I make a quick step toward him, he instantly forgets about being a "large emu/Goliath bird," and becomes a killdeer again, fleeing loudly for his life.

I haven't found their nest yet. I believe it is in the area of the shot put circle. I think this because both birds always lead me away from that specific area.

I've carefully looked in that area, but I've not found the nest. The small eggs blend in so well with the ground that I fear stepping on them while exploring the area

It is always amazing that any Killdeer young survive. Their nest on the ground is easy prey for predators. The young chicks cannot fly far. But regardless of this, you'll always see young birds in open areas yearly.

Once a pair laid their nest right among the gravel of our driveway. Day after day we drove right over the nest, which was centered between where our tires drove. After the young were hatched, they would still stay in that spot and scurry frantically as a car approached.

Now you *noticed* that I entitled this story as to why I believe in God... One of the reasons comes from watching the two Killdeer. No one has to teach these birds how to show the "broken wing limp" or the "inflated big bird shuffle." All killdeer, throughout their wide range over most of America, exhibit these same defense mechanisms to protect their young.

What they do is due to instinct. Some expert observers will explain that these actions are learned behavior developed through vast millenniums of evolutionary time. That is fine and good, but I'm just simple enough to believe that their Creator placed this instinct in them as He made them unique. This God-given instinct to protect the young is found in so many different ways throughout the wonderful animal kingdom.

Where others may see evolutionary development, I sense the large fingerprints of an organized plan, brought about by an Intelligent Master Designer.

> I call Him God…
> I see His handiwork everywhere.
> For me, it would take much, much more faith
> to believe that these things, even small things like the
> Killdeer's broken wing instinct and the chimney
> swift's clockwork navigation system are all an
> accident of evolution.

The Ripple Effect

*"Do all the good you can,
In all the ways you can,
In all the places you can,
At all the times you can,
To all the people you can,
As long as ever you can."*
-John Wesley

It was a wonderful day. The sixty-two members of our Dry Creek Camp family sat high in the upper deck near the left field foul pole at Houston's Minute Maid Park. We had traveled as a group for a fun weekend as a way of saying thanks to our wonderful summer staff.

There's nothing like walking into a major league ballpark. I love the scene from "The Rookie" where a team of high school players from West Texas enter the seating area at The Ballpark in Arlington, Texas. Their look of awe as they stand there is exactly how I felt the first time I was in a major league stadium.

I still feel the same wonder entering Minute Maid Park as the first time I stood under the vastness of the Astrodome roof as a child. I've watched this same excited feeling of awe on the faces of my own boys for over twenty years.

About half of our group is seeing their first major league game. We settle in our seats up in the "nosebleed" section as the Astros and Chicago Cubs prepare to play. Most of our group is pulling for the Astros. A few Cubs fans are mixed in. Gary Wiley Ashworth, one of our staff leaders is loudly pulling for the Cubs, mainly to aggravate those of us who love the Astros.

The game begins and it is an exciting one to watch. There are home runs, exciting plays, and a good old fashioned fight where Jeff Kent of the Astros and his manager get tossed out. The manager, Jimmy Williams, follows up his ejection by kicking dirt on home plate, much to the delight of the crowd, especially our Dry Creek staffers

Midway through the game, an event occurs that is even more memorable than the home runs or excitement of the game. Some of our crew decides they need to start a wave. They get together and Thomas Bethke, our most extroverted staffer, decides to start the wave from his end row seat in the upper deck.

The wave begins at Minute Maid Park

Minute Maid Park is not conducive to good waves. There are few seats in the outfield areas. Because of this it is hard to make a 360 degree circle of a crowd wave. Getting a wave with sustained momentum is next to impossible. But that doesn't deter Thomas and our staffers. They begin to stand and yell as they raise their arms. Their first attempts barely make it out of our section.

Personally, I don't care for waves. I've come to see a ballgame and don't want a bunch of people standing up and hollering just as Jeff Bagwell steps to the plate. Even so, trying to be a good team player, I take part in the wave.

All sixty-two of our crew are now avidly taking part in the wave. Small groups of fans throughout the upper deck stands take part.

After many attempts with only small success, I expect our wavers will give up and return to the game at hand. But I've underestimated our staffers: They are determined to have a good stadium-sweeping wave.

Now on each successive try, Thomas and our crew see momentum build on each wave. It's mainly on the upper levels, but it does travel around about two thirds of the stadium. Our crew continues to start each wave off with enthusiasm and cheering.

The wave continues to grow and then, to our amazement, it makes its way completely around Minute Maid Park.

Thinking on it later I realize that this wave, in one way or another affected a crowd of 42,679. It was started by one person, our boy Thomas. He was then joined by those around him, and then others, until the entire crowd joined, and even those diehard fans (like me) who detest crowd waves still had to acknowledge that it was a fine wave.

And I thought about our ministry at Dry Creek Camp. What God does in the hearts of campers, especially teens, can have a ripple effect that can never be completely measured or predicted. At the camp we have a saying that describes the ripple effect of our camp ministry:

Only Heaven will reveal the lives that have been changed, by the lives that have been changed, by the lives that have been changed by the Lord at Dry Creek.

When God starts a good work, He continues it and finishes it. Each life changed by His love bumps against, and intersects with other lives. Just as when a rock is tossed into the water, the resulting ripples travels far and wide.

I saw a reminder of this "ripple effect" last year in China during a visit in the home of Chris and Annette Place. They are serving the Lord though the ministry of Hope Medical Center in Macau Province. Chris, a medical doctor, works with the residents of this Baptist clinic. Annette is busy with their six precious children (three Chinese and three Americans.) They live on the 31st floor of a huge towering apartment complex.

Sitting there with them, I recalled Annette's years as a student at East Beauregard High School. She was one of my students. She was a wonderful learner and fun to teach. She came from a good country family. Her dad was our game warden and her mother worked at the school as a teacher's aide.

...And here was this Sugartown girl serving God halfway around the world. As we visited, and what a special visit it was, Annette reminded me of two things. First of all she told me,

"Coach Iles, you probably don't remember it, but my life was changed when I met Jesus at Dry Creek Camp as a camper."

That thrilled me, but Annette wasn't through, "A few years later as a youth camper, I first heard God's call upon my life toward missions. And here I am today in China!"

Once again I could see that water ripple from a rock spreading all the way across a large body of water, in this case the vast Pacific Ocean.

It was an emotional moment as Annette shared this. I smiled through my tears and replied, "Well, Annette that decision sure brought you a long way from Sugartown and Dry Creek, didn't it?"

A few months after this China trip, I talked to one of my camp manager friends in Texas. Eric Small is the manager of Piney Woods Baptist Encampment, a wonderful camp south of Lufkin. He told of encountering a young man in a Target store in College Station. This man was a cadet at Texas A & M. The student saw Eric's camp shirt and inquired as to where he worked. After Eric finished telling about Piney Woods Camp, the student said, "Well, I met the Lord at a little camp over in Louisiana. You've probably never heard about it, but its name is Dry Creek."

Once again, that ripple from a distant rock amazed me at how God works...and works and works.

The ripple effect doesn't have to go across the Pacific Ocean, or even across the Sabine River to be effective. Part of our ministry at Dry Creek is to get out into the world right where we are. This neat story from the summer of 2003 illustrates this "stay at home" principle:

During the summer I don't watch much television, so I didn't see the news on this July weekend. But plenty of other folks saw this story on KPLC Channel 7. The news featured a story on a large drug bust in Lake Charles. Their main video of the arrests showed a big man being put in a squad car. You've seen enough detective TV shows to know how they carefully guide the head of the handcuffed suspect while they placed him in the back of the squad car.

What everyone saw, and couldn't wait to call me about, was that this handcuffed older man had on a bright blue Dry Creek Camp T-shirt.

At first this embarrassed me, and we were the butt of plenty of joking the rest of that week. Then I realized that the fact that this man had on a Dry Creek shirt meant that the gospel of Jesus had penetrated somehow into this man's family. Jesus said it best in Luke 4:18:

"The Spirit of the Lord is upon me, because he hath anointed me to preach the gospel to the poor; he hath sent me to heal the brokenhearted, *to preach deliverance to the captives,* and recovering of sight to the blind, to set at liberty them that are bruised." (King James Version),

I'm sure this man's son had attended one of our camps. It was a reminder that the ripples God starts will penetrate into areas we would never expect.

The following historical event helps illustrate the power of "the ripple effect":

On August 27, 1883, one of the greatest volcanic eruptions in history took place on the island of Krakatoa, located near the Indonesian island of Java.

In one tremendous explosion the entire island was blown sky high and the world was never the same. What was so amazing about this eruption was the effects it had over the entire planet.

In his book, *Krakatoa*, Simon Winchester tells of the long term world-wide effects of this volcanic explosion. ... The shock wave from Krakatoa's final cataclysmic explosion had traveled around the earth not once but seven times.

In the Ceylon town of Panama, 2000 miles away, a woman died when she was swept from the harbor rocks by an immense influx of water. This tidal wave was traveling at 370 mph.

In the harbor of Socoa, France, 10,729 nautical miles from Krakatoa, there were seven small waves that traveled up the English Channel, from this original wave in the Pacific.

The millions of tons of dust hurled into the upper air in the East Indies disseminated themselves around the world for many years and caused all manner of extraordinary phenomena- not the least of which were sunsets. These brilliant sunsets, caused by the dust particles blown out from Krakatoa, were the delight of viewers and landscape painters for up to two years.

The temperature of the earth was also cooled by the volcanic dust in the atmosphere. The haze resulted in a drop in temperature of one degree worldwide.

One single event in the vast Asian hemisphere affected conditions around the world.

Now, who knows what will happen when another "Annette," or an "Andy", attends camp this summer at Dry Creek. Maybe four or five days in the environment of camp will be the location of a life-changing, world-altering experience with Jesus.

> A ripple, whether small or large,
> that starts in Dry Creek,
> and travels around the world
> affecting an entire city, a vast nation,
> or even the entire planet.

> Don't underestimate God..
> And don't underestimate what can happen when a young person personally experiences the love and power of God in their life.

> It's called the ripple effect...

Krakatoa by Simon Winchester
Copyright 2003 HarperCollins Publishers

"Trail Magic"

Have you ever heard of the term, "Trail Magic"?
Here is a story that best describes it:

Frank Bogard and I walked along a rocky section of the Appalachian Trail, (or the "A.T." as it is called) in North Georgia. The day before we had climbed (well, Frank climbed, I more or less actually crawled) over Blood Mountain. The mountain got its name from a famous battle between the Cherokee Indians and another tribe. But "Blood Mountain" meant to me that I thought I was going to die.

But thanks to Frank's patience and encouragement, we made it. Today's trail, although still challenging, is much less strenuous.

It's early May and beginning to warm up. Even in the higher elevations that the AT traverses on its Southern end, the days are hot. I'm sweating profusely and ready to find a spring for some water.

In hiking you must choose whether to treat your drinking water or take a chance on its purity. The temptation is always to drink that cold spring water without using chemical tablets, but it is easy to become ill from this water that seems so pure.

So Frank and I always treat our water. The tablets give it a slightly bad taste that we try to cover with lemon juice. Additionally you are recommended to wait at least fifteen minutes before drinking. That is difficult to do when you're hot and thirsty.

I am thinking about this next drink of water knowing that both of my water bottles are empty.

With these thirsty thoughts in mind as we headed north on the trail, we spotted an orange container up ahead.

Coming up to it, we see that it is a five gallon water cooler. On it a simple handwritten note reads,

"Cold water. Enjoy! From a '79 thru hiker."

We can't believe it's true but when we press the spigot on the cooler, cold icy clear water comes forth. Frank and I drink our fill. I'm positive I've never tasted anything better in my life.

And the water is so good... but equally satisfying is the thought that some human, who has hiked this same trail from here in Georgia all the way to Maine, is thoughtful enough to leave an ice-filled cooler for hikers.

We look around for a road or four wheeler tracks, but see no easy access to this part of the trail. I wonder how our water carrier got to this spot, for he/she picked a very important spot. The trail guidebook reminds us that water is scarce on this section.

I think of the effort this kind soul put into bringing this water cooler to this particular spot. How often does he do this good deed? Will he be back today or tomorrow?

Although I'll never know this "Trail Angel" I raise my cup in tribute to this example of Trail Magic.

Before leaving we add to the scribbled thank you notes left on paper and held down by a rock.

Curt and Frank Bogard on Springer Mountain, Georgia, the southern end of the Appalachian Trail.

We leave there and travel up the trail with water bottles full of water. But just as importantly our hearts are lighter due to this generous act of Trail Magic.

Every AT hiker can attest to Trail Magic, especially those who make the entire 2000 mile trek in one season. On the other end of this trail, I experienced another example of trail magic in Maine.

My hiking partner, "Mac" Rathburn (aka "Snoring Thunder" and "Louisiana Man") had left the trail a few days earlier and I was to meet him in a trail town on Labor Day. I left the trail and began a long hike out. It was about fifty miles to the town of Monson where I would meet him at a boarding house for hikers.

I walked several miles of old logging road and then came to a more travelled gravel road. After a short spell on this road, I came upon a cabin. It was a simple but beautiful woods cabin sitting beside a crystal blue lake.

Even though it was early September, smoke curled up

from the chimney. It gets much cooler early in the higher elevations of Northern woods.

I was pretty turned around as to my direction back to the real world, so I approached the house, stepped up on the porch and rapped on the door.

The door opened to a sight that looked just like a Norman Rockwell painting. There sat an older man in a colorful flannel shirt with suspenders. Two generations of family sat around him at the breakfast table as a crackling fire burned in the fireplace. The smell of breakfast reached my nose on its way to my stomach.

I told them that I needed directions and everyone began at once to give me directions. The woman of the house got up and brought me two hot blueberry muffins with a cold glass of milk. As I ate like a ravished wolf, one of the men wrote out directions on a napkin.

I thanked them profusely, quickly took their offer of two more muffins "for the road" and started walking again. It was still twelve miles to the highway and I hoped I might catch a ride.

I had just finished the last muffin when an old brown Ford truck roared up behind me. It was one of the guys from the blueberry breakfast house. He told me to hop in. He insisted on taking me all of the way to the highway.

We visited as he drove across the rough mountain road. We never encountered another vehicle and I realized I probably would have walked the entire twelve miles without his act of Trail Magic.

My last experience of receiving this gift called Trail Magic comes from the middle part of the AT. Last year my son, Clint, his friend Chris Jones and I took a hike through the Smoky Mountains of Tennessee/North Carolina. We arrived at a shelter one night after dark. The moon showed enough light allowing up to slip into the shelter without disturbing the four or five sleeping hikers with our flashlights.

This trail shelter was the famous "Fontana Hilton." Located at the southern entrance to the Great Smoky Mountains National Park, it is much nicer than the usual shelter. It is newer, cleaner, and free of mice. It sits next to Fontana Dam which bridges the Little Tennessee River. To enter the park, you actually walk the roadway across the top of the dam to continue on the AT through the Smokies.

As we laid out our sleeping bags and crawled in, a sleepy hiker said, "Tomorrow morning there'll be pancakes and sausage at the parking lot next to the dam."

Everyone was up early the next morning. As we carried our packs down to the trail and to the parking lot, we saw a RV with about six scruffy hikers gathered around. Two guys were cooking breakfast. One was outside cooking sausage on a Coleman stove. The other guy was going in and out of the RV, each time returning with a heaped plate of hot pancakes.

It was obvious these two cooks were enjoying cooking and serving the breakfast nearly as much as the hikers were enjoying being the recipients of this act of trail magic.

The two guys were from Ohio. They were postal workers who had taken their vacation to cook and serve the thru hikers passing through here on their way north. All they expected for the breakfast was a chance to share a short scripture and prayer. In fact their ministry was called, "Hikers for Christ."

We all commented on what a neat ministry they had -helping out hikers - just for the pure joy and ministry of it. Isn't that what it's all about?

After experiencing Trail Magic in various parts of our nation, I've come to a conclusion that these types of acts of kindness are not "southern hospitality", but rather "rural hospitality."

There is something about living in places where you personally interact with people and they become a real individual, not just a face in a crowd of hundreds that brings out the best in people. Trail Magic is just the natural byproduct of people being together in an environment where someone becomes an individual, not just one more face in a sea of humans

Sad to say, but acts of Trail Magic are harder to come by in the big cities, regardless of their geographical location. Whether it's New Orleans or New York City, the impersonal nature of city life takes away from people's willingness to risk and show some "Trail Magic" to a stranger.

Trail Magic—it doesn't have to be limited to the Appalachian Trail.

It is simply the art and habit of looking for ways to make a person's load lighter and their smile brighter.

Let's practice it together.
            Trail Magic... Make it a habit.

The Coach and the Ref

In one of my former lives, I was a coach. I coached basketball and baseball and really enjoyed every part of it.

I'm still a coach, although my "court" is now different. Coaching is all about leading, motivating and encouraging people. It involves helping them get the very best possible out of themselves, their talent, and seeing a group of individuals become a team

The following event actually took place during a basketball game at Pitkin High School. Although they are not named, "Coach" and "Ref" are two of my friends (at least they were before this story was published.)

The gym at Pitkin is a formidable place to play or coach. In addition to having excellent teams, their fans act as a "sixth man." They are not the least bit shy about insulting a coach, harassing a player or doing anything to help their Tigers win.

In the gym there is a corner of the stands commonly called "Amen corner." It is where, for as long as I have either played or coached there, a large group of men sit and "hold court." This group of tobacco chewing men always was quick with a verbal jab, directed to a straying ref or an opposing player.

And "Amen Corner" is right where the story of the Coach and the Ref culminated. It was in the final minutes of a hotly contested boy's game, Pitkin was pulling away and their lead was large enough so that everyone knew Pitkin would win. The opposing coach, who led the Broncos team, had worked hard, sweated, and done everything he could to coax his boys to victory.

The coach and the three refs had kept up a constant patter throughout the game...probably no more than usual for a high school basketball game. One of the refs, a balding man, received most of the criticism when he'd run by the bench.

As the clock ticked down and Pitkin's lead gradually increased, the Coach called what is termed as "a frustration timeout." There is no chance of winning but you want to stop and make a point to someone.

I once saw a NCAA game where a coach asked for a timeout with less than ten seconds remaining and his team down by 16 points.

As the college coach excitedly talked and drew on his clipboard, the announcer dryly said, "Well it looks like he's working on a 17-point play."

Now, back to our story in the Pitkin gym - As Coach called a timeout, he would have needed that same type of "double digit" play to come back and win. But that wasn't his reason for the timeout.

His tired, sweaty players stood with their hands on their knees. Coach leaned in and said, "Guys there's one person on this court who has killed us all night long. I want to know if any of you are man enough to guard him?"

As the coach looked into the eyes of his players, they all momentarily forgot their fatigue and glanced at each other. Finally the team's point guard, Adam, stepped forward and said, "Coach, I'll do it."

Adam was one of those players who made up in hard nosed plays for what he may have lacked in talent. He was the type of player usually described as, "He'd run though a brick wall if you told him to, and showed him which wall." So, it was no big surprise to anyone that Adam stepped forward.

He looked down the court to the Pitkin bench and asked, "OK, Coach, which one is he?"

Now I know you are probably a step ahead of me on this story, so let me catch up.

Sure enough, Coach was pointing at the bald-headed ref. As he pointed he added, "Yep, he's killed us all night long. Adam I want you to go guard him."

Adam incredulously looked and then the exclaimed, "Coach, do you really want me to guard that referee?"

"Yes, wherever he goes, you get down in your defensive stand, shuffle along, and guard him close.

With that the horn blew, followed by the referee's whistle and both teams broke their huddles.

Our Ref had moved to the sideline on the far end, away from the main action.

As fate would have it he had positioned himself right by the "Amen Corner." The guys in the corner saw Adam coming long before Mr. Ref did.

They watched with fascination as Adam got down in his defensive stance...knees bent, back straight, dominant foot back, hands up, feet sliding...with his eyes on the man he was "guarding." That's just about the same time Ref noticed Adam near him.

Mr. Ref did what anyone would do in the same situation - he trotted to one side, but he was blocked off by Adam's sliding feet. Probably a good head fake and body spin would have gotten Ref around Adam and into open court, but he was a little rusty on his "getting open" moves.

So Adam had him momentarily trapped in the corner, right in the Amen Corner...right by a group of men who were enjoying this scene immensely.

Most of the fans had not even noticed the "one on one" contest; they were involved in the action around the ball on the other end. But Adam's teammates on the floor as well as on the bench kept an eye cocked on Adam and the Ref's duet ballet.

Just about this time was when the Ref came to his senses and called a quick technical on Adam.

They said he was mad and red-faced as he stormed to the scorer's table to report the foul. Most of the gym didn't even know what had happened....

...but Coach did
...And Ref did
...And Adam surely did.

...But most of all the men over in the Amen Corner remembered...and still do...I don't even know what the final score was... or what happened next with Adam.

...If you're ever at a game at Pitkin, look for them over in the northwest corner... for a group of country men on the first two rows sitting like a jury awaiting a trial...ready to coach, encourage, berate, second-guess, and get their money's worth.

And if the action gets slow or a play is stopped for halftime, and one of the men stands and walks to the court edge and gets down in an uncomfortable looking stance as if he is guarding an imaginary player...and all of the other men blurt out laughing...you'll know why...it's just the men over in the Amen Corner reliving the night Coach told Adam to go guard the Ref.

Amen.

Available (but Unused) Power

I was born during a period of history when many World War I veterans were still alive. Of all those old men, the one that sticks out was a veteran named Manuel "Curt" Green.

Curt Green was one of those country men who had never been anywhere, nor desired to, until World War I broke out. He traveled across, as he called it, "The Big Pond" to France in the "Great War" to end all wars.

After the war ended he returned to Dry Creek and probably never traveled over a hundred miles from home for the rest of his life.

As a lifelong bachelor, he lived with his dogs near the home of his neice and her husband, Corine and Jay Miller.

Growing up, every time I would see Curt Green he was invariably driving his old Ford tractor, pulling a homemade trailer full of dogs. I would see him along the highway or at Ryan Harper's store. The dogs, usually five or six of them, would be yapping, barking, and having the time of their lives. (In Dry Creek the term "treated like a dog" doesn't always represent a bad life. I've seen plenty of dogs that were treated just like one of the family.)

On this old beat up tractor he never traveled much over ten miles per hour.

Later in life, maybe because of a pension or veteran's benefit, Curt Green bought a new vehicle. It was a light green 1969 Datsun truck. This was the first of the small pickup trucks. These trucks were made fun of by country men, both young and old as "made out of Japanese tin cans." Little did we know that these foreign vehicles would one day be the best made and most expensive available on the market. (Datsun is the company that later became Nissan.)

Curt Green's truck had a five speed manual transmission, but I never saw him get out of second gear. He was comfortable with going the same speed he'd always gone on his tractor.

He still hauled his dogs, only now they rode in the back of the truck. We could still pass him up on our bicycles, except that we felt like it was more of a feat due to his mode of travel being a truck rather than a tractor.

So in the remaining years of his driving life, Curt Green puttered along in his truck... never getting out of second gear when he had five... and never topping over twenty miles per hour.

As I think about Curt Green's green truck, I believe there is a life application - As followers of Jesus we have been given a promise of power. Power to live victoriously, power to overcome as He overcomes through us. This is so clearly presented in John 15 where Jesus tells His followers:

"Without me, you can do nothing."

Now we can do things, even plenty of good things, in our own power. But to do things that change lives and affect our eternity, it must be God's power working in us, and through us.

As Christians our job is simply to be a conduit for the "Living Water." Our job as a pipeline for carrying God's gospel is clear.

Once again, I must go back to the Appalachian Trail for an example. In the 100 Mile Wilderness in Maine, there is a famous shelter called Rainbow Springs. It is well known for its location, swimming area, due to it being featured in a National Geographic article from 1987.

As we approached the shelter we had to walk across a long log over the stream. It was late evening and a camp fire was already burning while a whole host of hikers were already there cooking supper, rubbing their sore feet, and comparing notes on the day's hike. It reminded me of scenes from the hobo jungles of the Great Depression years.

Of all the sights and sounds I remember from my overnight stay at Rainbow Springs, one image stands out. Adjacent to the shelter was a large beech/birch tree. Into the bark and wood, someone had carved out a neat rectangle and placed an electrical socket. It just fit right into the tree and looked as if it was ready for use. One bearded hiker even commented, "If I'd known that was here, I would have brought my electric razor!"

What made the electrical socket such a neat conversation piece was the fact that we were many, many miles from any road, much less any electrical power. In fact the only way in and out of this remote area was by this trail, or by the float planes that landed daily on the nearby beautiful large lakes of central Maine.

You see, an electrical socket is a great thing to have, but it is useless if it is not connected to a power source.

If we really want to be a difference maker, and that is why God has placed us here, we must be plugged into the source - our Lord Jesus.

Whether it's like the Rainbow Springs electrical socket - it looks good but is useless... or like Curt Green's Datsun truck - plenty of available five-speed, tire spinning power, but never used even close to its potential, we must be sure to use the available resources ready for us..

And my God will meet all your needs according to his glorious riches in Christ Jesus. Philippians 4:19

"Best Seat in the House"

> Oct. 19, 1996
> "A pine knot fire crackles in front of me; a cool breeze rustles foliage that is just going crimson and gold.
> A half moon glistens overhead and I am finishing my evening meal with hot cocoa and a chocolate bar.
> Somewhere to the north, fifty or sixty thousand people are packed into Yankee Stadium for the first game of the World Series.
> They paid more, but I have the better ticket by far..."

-Copied from a trail journal at Blue Mountain Shelter on the Ouachita Trail in Central Arkansas.

    I love the fine prose written by that unnamed hiker in Arkansas. As you've probably noticed many of my stories relate to the outdoors and nature. Please excuse me if I strike that "one note song" pretty often.

    It's just that out in the woods is when I feel closest to God. There is something about being among nature that causes even a non-believer in God to think that there is too much order all around to be totally by accident.

And when I'm out in the outdoors, walking and listening, stories just seem to come to me that I want to write.

Last spring when it was still cool and the mosquitoes, redbugs, and ticks had not yet become a nuisance, I was out in the woods on a late evening walk. As I came to Crooked Bayou, the stream along which my family's first homestead is, I sat down to watch the approaching darkness in the swamp. It was quiet and seems as if the whole world has taken a vow of silence as the night comes on.

Suddenly a far off Barred Owl called. This owl is our most common one and is smaller than its more aggressive cousin, the Great Horned Owl.

The Barred Owl has a distinctive eight note call, usually divided into two sets of four such as,

"Who cooks for you... who cooks for you alllll?"

This is how the old timers described its call. Some birders describe its call as "similar to the barking of a dog."

Sitting on the creek bank, I cup my hands over my mouth and do my best owl imitation. I'm happily surprised when my call is returned by the owl. We continue our "conversation" and soon his call comes closer and I know he is coming to investigate who the trespasser is on his personal property.

To the west, deeper in the swamp, another owl answers. We now have owls "in stereo."

With each series of hoots, the first owl is getting closer to where I'm sitting on the creek bank. The owl behind me to the west is still calling but has not changed its location.

When my owl friend hoots again, he is very close to my spot. I strain my eyes to look up in the surrounding beech trees to catch a glimpse of him. I know the direction he seems to be coming from, but I cannot spot him. My years of listening to owls have taught me that they have an uncanny way of seeming to throw their voice.

Finally, the owl flies into the tree directly over my head. An owl in flight surprises you with their broad wingspan. They are bigger than they seem to be when seen sitting on a limb.

There is still enough light to see the owl's silhouette. I sit quietly not willing to make any move or sound that would scare him away. The owl and his partner to the west continue their calling back and forth.

Yes, just like the unknown hiker from that Arkansas shelter on that cool October night, I also have "the best seat in the house."

I've got a front row box seat for the evening hoot owl concert.

As the dueling owls continue their chatting, I detect a more excitable song on the end of their calls. Dr. Lowery, in *Louisiana Birds* states, "…hoots are followed by a long drawn out weird scream that is enough to chill the bones of the initiated."

I agree about the spookiness of this scream. I don't know exactly what it means – whether it is a challenge to fight, or an invitation to come visit. Their mocking spooky calls end with my nearby owl flying toward the west and the other owl flying to meet him.

I wonder if they perform this rite each evening whether I'm there to eavesdrop or not.

It's much darker now and I get up to cross a small log across the creek and head back from the swamp to higher ground and my truck.

It is a good feeling to have just been out in the woods. No time schedule, no interruptions... just having the best seat in the house -   A front row seat at the evening hoot owl concert.

"Come to the woods, for here is rest." -John Muir

P.S. My friend at Blue Mountain Shelter predicted the Braves to beat the Yankees in six games. He missed it. The Yankees won the 1996 World Series 4 games to 2. On the night of his journal entry, the first game in New York City was rained out by a strong storm.

Hey, Mr. Tambourine Man

It is always a good day at Dry Creek Camp when Mackey Willis sits down at the piano. You can sense that everyone at this men's event is ready to worship and sing. As always, I know we'll have some fun... but most of all we'll sing praises to our great God.

Mackey's family joins him on the stage. As each one approaches their microphone or instrument, I see that Mackey has added a new member to the family singers. An older man is helped up onto the Tabernacle stage. I watch closely wondering if he might be a relative of Mackey's.

A second look tells me this man is blind. A man carefully seats him in a chair against the stage wall.

Then I see it - this man has a tambourine... And when the Willis family begins to sing, his instrument comes alive. Being a drummer myself, I love and appreciate the role of percussion in worship.

And this old man is good - His rhythm and timing are perfect. He knows just when to be ready for one of Mackey's unique changes in time or improvision. He is a wonderful addition to the already talented Willis family. The singing sounds extra good for there is nothing like hundreds of men singing in the Dry Creek Tabernacle. I always think, "This is what Heaven will be like!"

After thirty minutes of spirited singing, we dismiss to the dining hall to enjoy supper. I catch up with Mackey and ask, "Man, I like your tambourine player! Who is he?" Mackey looks at me with a quizzical smile and says, *"I don't have an idea in the world. I'd never seen him until he sat down behind me on the stage."*

Later, I find "The Tambourine Man." After greeting him, I comment, "You're good. It sounded as if you've played dozens of times with the Willis family." Our new friend grins and tells me, "Son, when I pick up that tambourine, God just takes over my hands. He is who I'm playing for." I believe Mr. Tambourine Man's statement is so true of how God wants to use the handiwork of our hands and hearts for His glory. We are all simply instruments in God's hands- ready and willing to be used, but helpless and unable to strike a "rhythm" until His Hand and Spirit moves upon us.

The works of a man or woman's hands are such special gifts because they are an expression of the soul and heart. I see this when I watch the skillful hands of musician, or an expert welder, or the practiced eye of a woodsman, who can "fall a tree" right where he wants it.

I think of the talented hands of my lifetime friend David Cole as he makes a beautiful saddle, or the tender yet hard hands of a loving older woman who has sewn a half century's supply of handmade quilts..

We can see it in the teacher's hands that have written a lifetime of math problems on a chalkboard... the doctor's skilled hands. Or the firm handshake of a man who has worked hard outside all of his life. Or the careful strokes of my Uncle Bill, a skilled artist as he puts onto canvas what most of us can only see but not replicate... Or his sister, my Aunt Margie, as she plays up and down the eighty-eight keys of the piano. She has no music in front of her, but ten hymnals full of notes and songs stored in her head and heart. What wonder!

All of these gifts of the hands, as well as the heart, are special treasures given to us by God. Yes, we work to develop these gifts. Many times this skill is the result of hours and years of practice and sacrifice. But no one should ever forget that these "gifts of the hand" are a treasure from God and it is only fitting that we express our appreciation and gratitude to Him.

A story is told of the famed Polish pianist, Ignace Jan Paderewski. During a concert tour of the United States he was scheduled to perform in a Midwestern city.

The concert hall was sold out and an air of anticipation could be felt as the well-dressed crowd filed into their seats.

All at once the crowd saw the form of a person approaching the grand piano which sat spotlighted in the center of the huge stage.

But it wasn't the grand master Paderewski. Instead it was a boy about seven years old. He strode to the piano and sat down. Many in the crowd thought that maybe this was an opening act featuring a new prodigy of the keyboard.

Everyone was amused when the boy began playing a typical seven year old's version of chopsticks. It was rough and he had to stop, back up, and restart several times. But it definitely was chopsticks.

Everyone was amused except one lady sitting on the aisle of the second row. The young boy playing the Steinway grand piano was her son. How he had escaped her attention and gotten on the stage was unknown but he definitely was her son and she was going to kill him when she got her hands on him. The embarrassment as to how he had ruined the start of the performance of the world famous pianist caused her face to redden.

Just then, as an entire concert hall sat in rapt attention, another figure strode across the stage to the piano. It was the grand master himself. The boy's mother felt as if she would faint.

What happened next is an illustration that not only was Jan Paderewski a great pianist, but also a caring human being.

He leaned over behind the seated boy and whispered into his ear,

"Just keep playing... don't stop... keep playing"

With that Paderewski began a beautiful two-handed accompaniment to "Chopsticks." The sight of the young boys beating out his two-fingered tune, as the great pianist reached around him to play along on each side of the keyboard was one that was never forgotten by anyone present that night.

And the duet was beautiful. It was music at its best.

The ovation was long and loud as the two pianists took bows together to the crowd.

That story is a clear example of the work by our hands. We approach our instrument, whatever that may be, and begin our simple little tune. Then our great God, if we allow Him, comes behind us and whispers, "Just keep playing... don't stop... let me join you."

And the resulting song is beautiful, and touching, and memorable.... All because just like my friend, The Tambourine Man, we allow God to use and guide our hands.

I am a depression survivor. I share that with you for only one reason: to encourage those in those in the darkness of depression that there is hope and light on the other side of this illness. This story is from my experience.

The Mockingbird's Midnight Song

It's the middle of another restless and sleepless night. It is a mind-numbing feeling to be exhausted physically and mentally, yet unable to get the thing you need most - sleep. Finally full of frustration, I get out of bed. That's what all of the sleep books tell you to do when you have insomnia: Get out of bed and do something. Read. Eat a snack. Watch TV. Pray.

I've tried all of these night after night and very seldom do any of them work. My mind and heart seem to be racing along at one hundred miles per hour. Nothing can seem to slow down this sadness and anxiety that is in me.

On this particular night, I decide to walk outside. It's about midnight, cloudy, and there is no moon. In the country, outdoor lighting is not as common as in the city. So my yard is very dark even as my eyes adjust to being outside. I've always loved being outside at night... looking at the stars, tracing the lights of an overhead jet, listening to the soothing sounds of the night.

But in my depression and insomnia, my soul feels just as black as the darkness surrounding me. I'm completely enveloped in it. I stand there trying to concentrate and pray in the quiet darkness. I think back to the books I've read by those who've been depressed. Those writers state something that I've found is common - they always describe their depression in terms of darkness, night, or blackness. One writer calls it, "The black night of the soul." Nobel Prize winning author William Stryon described it as "the black dog of despair." I understand this darkness all too well...

Tonight the silence is deafening. It is as if even the night creatures, such as crickets, owls, frogs, and barking dogs, have found a hiding place to escape the darkness.

Then suddenly from the river birch tree in our yard comes clear beautiful singing. It is a mockingbird. If you aren't from the South and haven't heard this bird, it is hard to describe its song. This song is loud and it is made up of about seven sequences of sounds - some stolen from other birds or nearby common sounds. I once read about a city mockingbird that could clearly mimic the notes of a traffic cop's whistle.

This bird in our tree is a real singer. She sits up high in the tree as the guardian of our yard. And she sings... and sings loudly... and with passion. To her, it doesn't matter that it is a dark moonless night when any respectable bird should be silently sleeping.

This mockingbird is going to sing even if it is midnight... Even if it is dark... Even if no one else hears her song. She is singing for the simple pure joy of singing.

...And the fact that she has the entire sound stage to herself makes her song seem louder and fuller. It is the end of the opera and the great diva soloist is singing her aria, she needs no accompaniment, and any other sounds would only diminish the incredible beauty of her solo.

This singing mockingbird unknowingly gives me a great gift... I'm reminded of how a person can sing... even in the darkness... even in tough circumstances.

Yes, I'm reminded by this bird, and really by the God who created both her and her song, that I will get through this time of darkness. There is still hope for the restoration of joy... and even though now it seems I've lost my song, it is still deep down within me... and one day will once again be sung loudly and joyfully.

... Now, I'd like to tell you my depression ended that night, but it would not be true. The mockingbird that sang at midnight was only one of a thousand steps on my road to restored health and joyful living. I firmly believe it was a gift from God just for me. It is a gift that I now pass on to you.

The gift of a mockingbird, in the darkness, singing at midnight

The entire story of this bout with depression, entitled *The Mockingbird's Song* can be ordered by visiting www.creekbank.net or contacting curtiles@aol.com.

"Aunt Mary Jane"

I grew up in a great place - the rural South. There are so many wonderful things about a country Southern upbringing. One of the best parts is the large extended family you grow up in. As a small boy I had a multitude of great grandparents, grandparents, great uncles and aunts galore, cousins, and every other kin folk in the world.

And on top of that I grew up with something else special - a whole host of older adults who filled the roles of surrogate grandparents. Most of these were addressed by the time-honored southern title of "uncle" or "aunt." I'd probably started school before I realized some of them weren't really a blood kin uncle or aunt.

I've never quit figured out at what age, and how it was decided when and who, would be known in Dry Creek community as "Uncle Johnny" or "Aunt Alice." Not every older person received this honorific title; instead, it was reserved for those kind souls that seemed to exist everywhere in our community.

It was a title of endearment and most of all a term of respect. To me, those we addressed as uncles and aunts were always given much honor by the younger people of our community.

I've found that this term of respect is not just limited to our Southern culture. Recently I was on a backpacking trip in China. As I studied the language books on Mandarin, the main Chinese dialect, I found that a word, *Ayi,* (pronounced *"eye-e,"*) is used toward an older woman of grandmotherly age. It means "respected aunt."

阿姨

*The Chinese characters for "respected aunt,"
pronounced "eye - e."*

Traveling through this rural area of SE China, we would encounter rural natives whom I suspect hadn't seen a non- Oriental face in their life. Some of the older women would stand up and quickly leave at the sight of a tall white backpacker came around the corner of their yard.

However, I quickly found that one simple word with a smile and nod was all the introduction needed. I would simply say "eye e" in my mangled Chinese to these women. A wide often toothless smile, set off by eyes full of wonder, would always be returned. Just like my Southern home half a world away, a term of respect was understood and accepted. A term of respect that I suspect wherever you would travel in the rural world, there would be an equivalent term for older men and women.

Here is a section from *The Mandarin Phrasebook by Lonely Planet* (4th edition):
"China's efforts to limit its vast population through their 'one child' policy is rendering several kin terms obsolete. Most Chinese no longer have uncles or aunts in the People's Republic, so the array of words for 'uncle' and 'aunt' are on the endangered list."

An older Chinese "ayi" (aunt) heads to the fields

How sad that, due to most families now having only one child, young people will not have brothers, sisters, uncles, or aunts. An important layer of society is being ripped out by these short-sighted policies.

While walking in China, I thought back to all of the ladies who had been respectfully called "Aunt" in Dry Creek...

Of all of them, one still stands out in my mind: Aunt Mary Jane Lindsey. Aunt Mary Jane was one of those who

Aunt Mary Jane Lindsey, a Dry Creek legend, at age 90.

transcended the Dry Creek area of the 19th century as well as the 20th century. Born in 1874, she lived until 1972. In my childhood, she was Dry Creek's most well known senior citizen. She lived, until age 98, in her old dogtrot home on the north side of the Longville gravel pit road.

As you can tell from her picture taken at age 90, she was a spicy lady with her own mind and unique way of doing things. Even in her old age she still lived alone and drove her car throughout the community.

There is one tale concerning her that may be Dry Creek community's most beloved story. In the days before paved roads in Dry Creek, travel and traffic was much slower. Due to this, many older people drove long past when they should have. Taking the car or truck keys from an older person was and still is a difficult task.

Well, no one in Dry Creek had been brave enough to take Aunt Mary Jane Lindsey's car keys, even though her driving skills had become weak at their best.

I remember my mom telling me as a boy, "Curt, if you're riding your bike along the road and see your great grand 'Pa,' or Mrs. Leila Heard, get in the ditch as fast as possible!"

Aunt Mary Jane either didn't have good brakes, or chose not to use them much. Dry Creekers told of her no holds barred driving style. Even though her driving days had ended by the time I knew her, I could imagine her unique personality behind the wheel of a car and it was not a pretty sight. In my preteen mind, I saw her just as this story goes:

Each day Aunt Mary Jane would drive to the post office to get her mail and go by the store. Evidently she would simply shift down to second at the stop sign before she barreled out onto the Dry Creek highway, which was not paved at the time of this story.

On this fateful day, she was making her arcing turn off Gravel Pit Road onto the main road. She didn't see the large loaded gravel truck barreling along northward toward her.

The dump truck driver was evidently a good driver. He didn't have much time or room to react when he saw the old car pull into his lane. But he did the best he could under the circumstances. He whipped his truck to the left trying to get around the slow car… and he nearly made it.

He clipped the side of the car and saw it spin round as it tumbled off into the ditch. His last view was of the old lady driver, hands glued to the wheel, eyes staring straight ahead.

As quick as he could, he got his loaded truck stopped. He sprinted back toward the car which was lying on its side in the far ditch. He was sure the old woman had been killed. It took him just long enough running back to the accident site for Aunt Mary Jane Lindsey to do two things: One, climb out of the overturned car, and secondly, figure out what in the world had happened. By the time the truck driver neared her, she was ready.

He was just glad to see her standing there alive and apparently uninjured. Aunt Mary Jane was waiting for him with her hands on her hips.

When he got close enough, she put her spindly finger right in his face and said, "Young man, every person in Dry Creek knows that I come out of this road every day at this same time going to the post office. You need to be more careful when you're driving in the future, especially when you come through Dry Creek!"

I wish I knew who the unlucky truck driver was. I'm sure he didn't have much to say after his tongue lashing. What could you say to a lady old enough to be your great grandmother who is airing you out?

Yes, I'm glad I grew up in Dry Creek. A place where a young person still has plenty of adopted aunts, uncles, and grandparents, and none more memorable than "Aunt Mary Jane" Lindsey.

The following is a different type of story from what I usually share. I have written it simply to serve as one more reminder of the generation of men and women who sacrificed to protect our nation's freedom in World War II.

A Soldier's Story

*Sergeant Leroy Johnson
U.S. Army   1941-1944*

*Every soldier has a story.
It's a story that needs to be told.
Some soldiers, often the bravest,
Never get to tell their story.
Then it becomes our job to tell their story...*

This is the story of Sgt. Leroy Johnson, United States Army.

Since 1965, a bronze plaque has stood on the median of Louisiana Highway 10 in the town of Oakdale. This plaque briefly tells the story of Sergeant Leroy Johnson. The inscription on the plaque ends with the wonderful words of Jesus from John 15:13,

*Greater love has no one than this,
that he lay down his life for his friends.*

Leroy Johnson was born on December 6, 1920 near Caney Creek, Louisiana. His father was a carpenter and his mother was busy rearing a large family of children.

While still a child, Leroy performed an act of heroism that would be a foretaste of his later brave deeds during World War II. When Leroy Johnson was nine, his first cousin, Elridge Hance, was visiting. Their moms, who were sisters, visited while the two cousins went exploring.

The boys came upon a freshly dug water cistern and decided to get a drink. Leroy and Elridge each got a Blackjack leaf and fashioned a folded water scoop. Leaning over the ten foot deep well, Elridge, age five, reached out too far and fell in.

Mr. Elridge, who now lives in Oberlin, told of going under several times, until Leroy grabbed him by the hair and held him out of the water. Leroy was too small to pull him out, but tenaciously held on until their mothers heard their yelling and came to the rescue.

Growing up, Johnson knew what is was like to work hard and do the best he could with what he had.

Men like Leroy Johnson, who later fought in our greatest war grew up in our nation's hardest time - the Great Depression. I've often thought that these difficult years prepared many of these future soldiers for being part of the victorious American armies that fought throughout Europe and the Pacific.

Many young men of this generation found work with the Civilian Conservation Corps. The "C.C.C. Camps" as they were called, gave these men jobs, some income (much of which had to be sent home to their families) and most importantly, a sense of self-respect and work skills. Additionally they learned to live and work together, a trait that came in handy during the next decade's war years.

Leroy Johnson worked in just such a camp in the Kisatchie Forest of central Louisiana. Lawrence Lacy, a Dry Creek area resident described his friendship with Johnson, "He was a good man to work with, and he liked to fight. We went at it more than once, but he was also a good friend to have."

In 1941, prior to Pearl Harbor and the outbreak of war, Leroy Johnson joined the Army. When he enlisted and was sent to boot camp, it was the last time he would ever be home in Allen Parish and see his family.

Evidently the Army agreed with him. From his letters home and comments from the men he served with, he was born to be a soldier.

He was placed in the 32nd Infantry Division. Most of the men in this Division were from the northern states of Wisconsin and Michigan. This division was involved in the large scale maneuvers then being held in the forests of Louisiana. New southern enlistees like Johnson were plugged into these units. I'm sure there were some interesting experiences from putting guys from the Louisiana woods with these Midwesterners.

From reading his service letters and the history of this division, we can track his travels over the next few years of the war. He was part of the campaign to take the eastern portion of New Guinea from the Japanese. This invasion was to stop the Japanese advance toward Australia.

General MacArthur stated his strategy when he said, "We will protect Australia from New Guinea."

Reading the official division history, it is learned that the fighting on this large island was difficult, slow, and deadly. The Japanese troops were experienced jungle fighters. The 32nd Division, which would later spend more days in actual combat than any other division in the war, was green and untried.

During this campaign was when Leroy Johnson first showed his prowess as a soldier. He was awarded the Purple Heart as well as the Silver Star for gallantry.

Sgt. Johnson spent part of the next year recuperating from his wounds in Australia

The 32nd division, or Red Arrow Brigade as its men called it, were part of the 1944 invasion of the Philippines. The fighting with the Japanese on the many islands of this country was tough and deadly.

Company K, in which Sergeant Leroy Johnson served, landed on the eastern Philippine island of Leyte. As they fought their way inland they came to an area near the Filipino city of Limon.

The commanding officer of Company K was Johney B. Wax. Captain Wax, also a Louisianan, had been Johnson's commanding officer for several months.

The brave act for which Leroy Johnson won the Congressional Medal of Honor is best described in the following two documents.

The first is the official Army citation of his heroism on December 15, 1944. The second is a transcript of a personal letter written by Captain Wax to Sgt. Johnson's parents shortly after the end of the war in 1945.

Official Citation: Congressional Medal of Honor

On 12/15, 1944 Sgt. Johnson was squad leader of a 9 man patrol sent to scout a ridge held by a well entrenched enemy force. Seeing an enemy machine gun position, he ordered his men to remain behind while he crawled within six yards of the gun. One of the enemy crew jumped up and prepared to man the weapon.

Quickly withdrawing, Sgt. Johnson rejoined his patrol and reported the situation to his commanding officer. Ordered to destroy the gun, which covered the approaches to several other enemy positions, he chose three men, armed them with hand grenades, and led them to a point near the objective.

After taking partial cover behind a log, the men had knocked out the gun and began an assault when hostile troops on the flank hurled several grenades. As he started for cover, Sgt. Johnson saw 2 unexploded grenades which had fallen near his men. Knowing that his comrades would be wounded or killed by the explosion, he deliberately threw himself on the grenades and received the full charge in his body. Fatally wounded by the blast, he died soon afterwards. Through his outstanding gallantry in sacrificing his life for his comrades, Sgt. Johnson provided a shining example of the highest traditions of the U.S. Army.

This following letter was sent to Johnson's family by Captain Wax:

October 16, 1945

Dear Mr. and Mrs. Johnson,
Several times during the last few months I have received good news, but none made me any happier than when I picked up last Monday's Times Picayune and learned that your son had been awarded the Congressional Medal of Honor.

He was a fine boy and every inch a soldier. I was closely associated with him for several months and always found him cooperative and helpful in every way. I witnessed the incident for which he received our country's highest award. After receiving his fatal wound, he managed to get up, take about three staggering steps and reach about three of us who were rushing up the hilltop to help him. We lowered him rapidly down the hill and he died within a few minutes.

Nothing can bring back his life but I am sincerely glad that a grateful nation could in some way, even though small, show their appreciation for what he did. His name hand the sacrifice he made will always stand out in a Division that has been outstanding throughout this war.

Johney B. Wax, Captain
Formerly C.O. Company K

(Captain Wax later served as long time principal at Live Oak High School where he touched many lives through the same leadership, concern, and discipline he exhibited as a company commander. He was present at the dedication of the Oakdale plaque on February 13, 1965. After a full life of investing in young people and bringing out the best in others, Johney Wax died in 1991.)

Leroy Johnson was buried near Limon, Leyte, Philippines with full military honors. At a later date, his body was moved to the American Military Cemetery near Manila, the capital of the Philippines. He is buried in plot C-10-79 along with 17,206 other brave soldiers. Among this vast number of graves are the remains of six other Congressional Medal of Honor recipients.

In addition, the New Orleans army base was renamed in his honor and memory as Camp Leroy Johnson. Although the base later closed, a bronze portrait of Sgt. Johnson once displayed at the base can now be seen in the Allen Parish Courthouse in Oberlin.

Thinking about Leroy Johnson's selfless act on that day sixty years ago, two questions come to mind:

First of all, when did he decide to fall on those hand grenades? Was it a split second decision where everything happened so quickly that all action was instinctive?

Then maybe Sgt. Leroy Johnson's act of laying down his life to protect his three fellow soldiers was not spontaneous. Could it have been a decision, or better yet, a commitment, he'd made days, even weeks, maybe months ago of what he would do in a situation like this?

Maybe he had sat around a battlefield campfire one night - the men of his company eating cold C rations, covered with mud. At that moment, he decided that he would gladly lay down his life for any of these men. Did he look around at these men gathered in a circle and think, "If I need to, I'm willing to die to save these men?"

Then my second question is maybe even more thought-provoking: What causes a man to throw himself, knowing sudden certain death awaits, on a hand grenade? In Sgt. Johnson's case, he outranked the three men with him on this patrol. Why was he, their leader, willing to die to save them?

My humble belief is that he did it because of love. Probably soldiers of Johnson's group would have been embarrassed at that term - "I did it because I love you."

But I go back to the words of the plaque in Oakdale. They are the words of Jesus, who also knew what He was talking about when discussing self-sacrifice:

"Greater love has no man than this- that he lay down his life for his friends."

I can think of no better way to say it and I will not attempt to put it differently. Jesus' words, as well as His actions, speak for themselves.

I guess one of the reasons I've always been fascinated by the story of Leroy Johnson is due to how his act in the Philippines is a reminder of what Jesus did on the cross for us.

Once again the leader, the "ranking soldier" in this unit saw that quick and decisive action was required. He did not appoint a lesser soldier to take action. He had been assigned this job by his commanding officer who watched from a short distance. He would finish this assignment - no matter what it took.

He freely, and willingly, took on the full brunt of the enemy's device. No one made him do it. He did it completely on his own.

Jesus freely sacrificed His life. Although there is no need for it, He would gladly do it again to save your soul. And a soul, the part of a human that lives on when this physical body dies and decays, is invaluable...and priceless... and worth whatever it takes.

> A soldier's story of sacrifice.
> A soldier's story to remember
> with both gratitude and respect.

"From Big D.C. to little d.c."

...Sometimes the best place to be is right where God has planted us."

The first time I heard about this future event I felt "called" to go. This call came during a meeting at the Houston Astrodome. 35,000 men were gathered, not to cheer the Oilers or Astros, but to worship, sing, and praise God. This two day men's event was sponsored by Promise Keepers, an organization started by former University of Colorado football coach Bill McCartney.

At the end of the Houston meeting, Coach McCartney announced that in two years there would be a huge Promise Keepers meeting at the National Mall in Washington, D.C. The name of the coming event was, "Standing in the Gap." This theme was based on the verse in Ezekiel 22:30:

"I looked for a man among them who would build up the wall and *stand before me in the gap on behalf of the land* so I would not have to destroy it, but I found none."

I turned to our guys in the Astrodome and stated that I was going, and from that day on I began to plan toward it. It was going to be a trip from my D.C. - a place called Dry Creek to the other D.C. - our nation's capital.

Many times we loosely use the term "I feel called by God...." We should use that term carefully and with reverence. But "called" is exactly what I felt on making this trip. I knew I would only be one person among hundreds of thousands, but if being one small raindrop in a flood of a million would help, I would do my part.

If my simple attendance in Washington, D.C. on an October Saturday would help our country regain its spiritual footing, I would gladly be there.

October 1997 finally came and eight men loaded up into two vans and headed northeast. One of the vans was mine and the other van, a Chevy Astro, belonged to a special friend, Jimmy Fisher of DeQuincy.

Driving eastward all night across the Deep South we were too excited to sleep. We were on a road trip and it was a road trip with purpose.

We hit Atlanta, Georgia the next morning at rush hour. My friend, De'Wayne Bailey was driving my van. Now, De'wayne is a pretty serious guy in any situation. But driving through downtown Atlanta at morning rush hour on I-85 was nearly too much for that Dry Creek boy. I still pick at De'Wayne about the grip marks he left on my steering wheel from his bumper to bumper Atlanta drive!

But by the time we reached mid-Georgia, there was serious trouble with the Chevy van. Jimmy's van was leaking transmission fluid badly. Traveling northward, we made more and more frequent stops where several quarts of transmission fluid were added.

By the time we reached Greenville, South Carolina, Jimmy finally said what we all already knew - He was going to be forced to stop and have the transmission replaced. Our first stop was at a Sears automotive store but no one could help us there. They sent us on to another shop. This was repeated several more times. By the time we reached the fourth, we were losing both our hope and an ever increasing stream of leaking transmission fluid.

This fourth stop was near the edge of town at a small transmission shop. Jimmy was visibly frustrated and tired as he went inside. He shared with the man at the front desk how he was from out of state and needed a rebuilt transmission put in. Knowing how far from home we were and being at the mercy of an unknown repair shop added to Jimmy's stress.

The man behind the desk quietly listened to Jimmy's plea and said, "Well, we'd like to help you but I'm not sure we can. We're closing down early today. All of us are going tomorrow to that men's meeting up in Washington, D.C."

Jimmy stood there stunned, fully knowing that not incredible coincidence, but rather God's leadership had brought him to this shop. Needless to say they quickly replaced Jimmy's transmission for a very reasonable fee.

Now with renewed excitement, our caravan was back on the interstate. During the day we began to mingle with buses, vans and cars of men, many of them decorated with sayings and scriptures- all headed northward toward our nation's capital.

That night we stayed in the Richmond, Virginia area. The next day, Friday, we arrived in Washington. We spent that day and most of the night seeing the sights around the National Mall. Everywhere you looked there were hundreds, even thousands, of men.

In the crowded Smithsonian Natural Science Museum, right under one of the huge dinosaur skeletons, I saw "Dog" Lambert from Merryville. I poked him from behind and said, "What's an old country boy from Beauregard Parish doing up here?" We laughed as we marveled at the odds of seeing a neighbor and friend here.

Several sights I saw that Friday are still vivid in my heart and mind - Inside the Capitol rotunda I saw three men face down on the marble floor weeping and praying for our nation. They lay prone right under the dome where the coffins of Presidents Lincoln and Kennedy had lain in state.

That night we stood on the steps of the lighted Lincoln Memorial as a lone saxophonist played "Amazing Grace." He stood up in the covered area by Lincoln's "seat." The echo of this beautiful hymn throughout the huge memorial was both eerie and touching.

On Saturday, the actual "Stand in the Gap" event took place... we rode the subway in from the Maryland suburbs. Everywhere there were men of every race, color, age and size. Many young sons walked beside their dads in a huge flow of men.

The National Mall is two and one half miles long from Lincoln's Memorial to the Capitol. It seemed as if every inch of grass or concrete had a man or boy standing on it.

I hate to admit it, but I barely remember the speakers or what was said. But every part of this day's experience was life-changing. It was just indescribable as to how it felt to be among this mass of humanity gathered to worship God.

We talk sometimes of "God speaking to us." That is something hard to explain or describe. I heard the story of how a wise old man told how God "had spoken to him." When asked if God had spoken in "an audible voice," the man smiled and replied,

      "Oh no, it was much louder than that!"

I would daresay that nearly every man present that day felt this special presence of God. I know it was sure true among our group of men. I'll always remember the moment as I knelt beside one of my former students, Greg Spears. A large flock of pigeons flew over the vast crowd. It was nearly a visible picture of how God's spirit was hovering over this gathering.

How did God speak to me? Well, like the earlier quote, it wasn't audible but it was deep in my heart. Here is what God showed me:

I had come to Washington to be among a vast crowd of men to "stand in the gap" for our country. From comparing the moral direction of our country to God's unchanging standards, I felt (and still do) a sense of concern.

But what God showed me was not a message of despair. Standing there in "Big D.C.," God kind of took me back to "my d.c." - the special place where I have lived, worked, and raised my family.

That day on the National Mall I realized that my calling - my place to stand in the gap - was a place called Dry Creek. A place where thousands of young people come yearly to have a fresh encounter with God. A place where marriages are healed and families strengthened.

I saw that the best place for me to take a stand was right where I was. On that day in front of our Capitol, I was willing to go wherever God wanted to send me—I would even come live in a big city like Washington if that was what God wanted. (I would go, but it might take a burning bush to convince me that my marching orders were correct.)

However, I saw with the eyes of my heart, that my place of service- *"my gap to stand in"* - was Dry Creek, Louisiana, USA. My calling was, and still is, to be available to join with God where He is working… and the camp where I serve is definitely a place where I see God at work.

This is the story I took home in my heart, and seven years later I still feel the same way. I hope I'm always ready to go where He leads and willing to serve passionately where He places me.

For now, God has placed me at Dry Creek Camp. I have been privileged to be part of this special place in every capacity from the trash boy to the manager. I've witnessed so many lives touched and re-directed. I count myself among those teens who have made commitments to God at camp and found their lives to never be the same again.

May it be said of each one of us that we stood in the gap and were found faithful, regardless of our level or place of service. Let us be faithful, whether it is in "Big DC" (our nation's capital) or "little d.c." - that place sitting at the intersection of two rural Louisiana highways, seemingly in the middle of nowhere.

"Being confident of this, that He who began a good work in you will carry it on to completion until the day of Christ Jesus." -Philippians 1:6

The Clear-Cut

Turning down the one-mile road to the home of my parents, my eyes and attention are once again riveted on what I call "The Clear-cut." This first half mile of Clayton Iles Road was populated by tall pines that had stood proudly since my childhood. I do recall when they were smaller, but they had been a part of our roadside for the forty years I've traveled along this road.

But this seventy-three acre tract of tall swaying majestic pines is gone. Earlier in 2003, they clear-cut the entire stand. Every pine was harvested and the once stately trees have now been replaced by an open field of stumps and weeds. Now there is nothing but a stark moonscape of stumps and rotting limbs. As if in further insult, the loggers left a few spindly tall pines along the small creek that flows through the field. Then as often happens with absentee landowners, once the trees were harvested the owners put the tract up for sale.

I stop my truck to look across the open field. Rolling down my window, I can no longer hear the beautiful sound of the north wind blowing through the pines... I think about the way pine limbs look when exposed to a brisk wind... The pine straw has a silvery look to it as they blow in the wind. An old song Daddy always sang comes back to me in snatches,

> *Whispering pines, whispering pines*
> *Where has she gone?*
> *Whispering pines, whispering pines,*
> *You're the one who knows.*

I recall stories of my great-grandparents describing the virgin Longleaf pine forests of Beauregard Parish: "The trees were so tall and thick that all underbrush was crowded out. Each year after the woods were burned, a thick new carpet of pine needles would blanket the ground. Even our wagons rolled along quietly under the cathedral of these tall 'Yellow pines.' "

Now, looking out the truck window I think, "I sure hope the next owners will come in and plant pines, so we watch the field once again become a stand of Louisiana pines."

This week my son Clint is working in the woods delivering pine seedlings to forestry sites. He tells of the amazing number of pine seedlings that the Mexican migrant workers can hand plant in a day. I realize that the timber companies and landowners are intent on replanting these areas for future income.

This reminds me that in spite of the clear-cuts, new growth takes place, and old fields again become full of beautiful pines. This cycle of birth, growth, and eventually death is true in all areas of nature. It is a cycle that we cannot stop, or even control. Like the weather, we must adapt to it, fully knowing it has no intention of adapting to us.

I remember another clear-cut a few years earlier when the timber company took the pines adjacent to the home of my parents. Daddy was then about age fifty-five. He stated matter of factly, "Well, I know I'll never see big pines in that field again."

Whatever becomes of this new 2003 clear-cut, it will always remain a measuring stick for me. Because right after these pines were harvested is when my father died. Looking out at the desolate and sad open field, I'm reminded of the barren spot in my heart due to the loss of this special man I called "Daddy."

In five years, ten years, or even twenty years, I'll look at the growing pines in this field and remember that my dad's death, in 2003, predated them. I know even when I am an old man, if God gives me a long life, I'll think about my dad when I see this field of pines. And I know I'll still miss him, no matter how long it's been or how tall the pines have grown.

I've heard so many men say, "My dad has been dead twenty-five years and I still miss him just as much as the day he died." Or "My father's been gone for three decades, and I still think about talking to him when I face a tough problem."

No matter what happens to that field - whether it stays open until the Tallow trees and Myrtle bushes take over, is used as pasture for cattle, horses, or replanted in Slash pines, I'll gauge the field by 2003-- the year my dad died... at the same time the clear-cut occurred.

As I continue down Clayton Iles Road, there is another change I'm aware of. I'm now driving on a paved road. It is the one thing I wish Daddy could have lived to have seen - the paving of the road to his house. Who'd have thought this would ever happen! Last year, Greg Nothnagel, our police juror, told dad of the pending paving. Daddy replied, "Well, I never thought I'd live to see the day our road was paved."

...Well, he didn't quite make it.

This newly paved road is special. It's the road of my childhood - the road I learned to ride a bicycle on with Daddy running along beside me.

It's the same gravel road that became slick and nearly impassable during long rainy spells in winter. I remember once when our car slid off in the ditch just about where the clear-cut now ends. It was late at night and I awoke in the back seat to hear mom and dad talking, as we sat there hopelessly mired in the mud.

Daddy left and walked the half-mile to the house, returning with a wheelbarrow to bring Colleen and me to the house. He wrapped us in a blanket against the cold night air. Mom was pregnant with my youngest sister Claudia as she trudged along beside my dad who was pushing the wheelbarrow full of two preschoolers. What a strange sight we must have been in the darkness of this cold Dry Creek night.

I think about how my ancestors, who settled this homestead in the nineteenth century, would respond to a paved road right up to their house. They would probably not even recognize the trails they had once traveled on.

This paved road is the same gravel road where I would walk at night as a teenager, kicking rocks as I tried to figure out the mysteries of life and girls. It's the same road I learned to drive a car on, trying to stay out of the ditches. This one-mile long road that led to the homes of my parents and grandparents was where the world was simple and I knew I was always welcome.

Because it was a dead end road with only the Iles clan at the end, the sound of an approaching vehicle always caused us to stop what we were doing and see what car or truck would round the curve. We knew the specific sounds of each family vehicle and could predict with pretty consistent accuracy who was driving up the road.

We always laughed, "If someone's coming down our road, they are either coming to see us, or lost." Now, this road has been paved, and the woods along the north road side have been cut and my dad, who loved this road because of the people who lived at the end of it, is also gone.

Reaching The Old House, I walk through the silent rooms filled with empty chairs. I think about the traditional verses of "Will the Circle be Unbroken":

> *You can picture the happy gatherings,*
> *'Round the fireside so long ago,*
> *And you think of their departing,*
> *When they left you here below.*
>
> *In the joyous days of childhood*
> *They often told of wondrous love*
> *They pointed to the dying Savior,*
> *Now they dwell with him above.*

I go through the rooms where the double fireplaces are. Old weathered rocking chairs sit in front of the cold hearth. The armrests are worn and stained from use by the generations of my grandparents and great grandparents. All of those loved ones are gone, but I remember them sitting in these rooms. I stop and recall each of them one by one - My precious grandmother, MaMa Pearl, who passed on a Godly heritage to me. Then I lovingly think of my maternal grandparents, who gave me that same heritage from their side.
. . . Now their chairs are all empty.

Now the first seat of that next generation is unoccupied. My dad's seat is now empty. I think of my precious aunts and uncles and how I love all nine of them and hate to think of one day losing them. Each of them are so much more than just an aunt or uncle.

Then I recall the third verse of that old song:
One by one their seats were emptied...
One by one they all went away...
And the family is now parted,
Will it be complete one day?

Will the circle be unbroken?
Bye and bye Lord, bye and bye
There's a better place awaiting
In the sky, Lord, in the sky.

Then I remember that I have faith. A faith that tells me that this is not the end. A fresh story pops into my mind. I just heard it last week, but I know I'll be telling it for the rest of my life:

A little girl was thrilled to find a bird nest in the bushes of her back yard. She ran to get her older brother to show him. Peering into the nest they saw six small blue speckled eggs.

The girl forgot about the nest for several weeks. Later when she went back to the nest, all she found were broken eggshells. Crying, she ran to find her brother. "The eggs are broken and there's nothing there" she sobbed.

The older brother went with her to the nest. Seeing the empty eggshells, he told her,

"But sissy, all that's left are just pieces of the shells, you see, *the best part has done taken wings and flown away."*

Then I recall the final verse of that old song:
When our loved ones who are in glory
Whose dear thoughts you often need
When you close your earthly story,
Will you join them in that place?

Then once again, I cherish that warm and precious gift God gives us - a memory of all of those good times, the good things, and best of all, those good people who affect our lives ... long after they've "taken wings and flown away."

Yes, the joys of memory...
... visible in a clear-cut field,
... beside a paved road.
... Even in an old empty house.

An eternal heart full of family and memories, all found along this one-mile road... A special road - special because of the people who have lived at its end.

"Whispering Pines" written by Johnny Horton.

"Will the Circle Be Unbroken" written by A.P. Carter (Public Domain)

The Old House   Dry Creek, Louisiana

Epilogue: "Happy and Sad"

As we conclude this journey together at the end of another book, I want to thank you for walking along beside me. The fact that you've made it to the end of this book tells me these words and stories must have touched you in some way (unless you just flipped to the back pages.)

Writing this book has been a journey for me. Your reading it makes it part of *your* journey.

My deep desire and wish is that this book has been a good companion during this stage of your life. If you are going through a difficult time, which we all experience, I hope these stories have encouraged you.

If your current journey is smooth and unencumbered, I hope my writings have helped you look all around and count, with gratitude, the many, many blessings you are now enjoying.

Recently I spent four days hiking in North Carolina. I had looked forward to this trip for weeks. In my pack I put a copy of the manuscript that would later become the book you are now holding.

I eagerly anticipated walking in the mountains during the day and then spending quiet evenings at campsites writing and reading.

But all of those plans changed on my first day as I left Max Patch, a beautiful grassy mountaintop north of the Smokies. My writing plans changed when I met "Wild Thing."

His real name was Bill and he was a retiree from California. He'd been given the trail name, "Wild Thing" during the last twenty-five days of hiking the Appalachian Trail beginning at Springer Mountain in Georgia. During this time he had covered over 250 miles, much of it over rough mountainous terrain.

He'd made friends among the many college-age thru hikers ("thru hikers" are those brave souls who attempt to walk from Georgia to Maine on the Trail. This five month trek of over 2000 miles is completed by only about one out of every ten who start in the spring.)

The day I encountered Wild Thing on the mountaintop at 4500 feet he was walking slowly and exhibited all of the signs of a discouraged hiker. I briefly visited with him and then he went on. I didn't expect to see him again as I was in no hurry.

But several miles down the trail I came upon him again. Wild Thing was sitting by a stream. We talked and he shared how he had walked alone for several days and was very lonely. He had decided to leave the trail and return home when he reached the next trail town of Hot Springs, North Carolina.

Sitting there talking, I thought about all of those half-written stories in my backpack needing work. But I knew that I was in the presence of a fellow traveler who simply needed a friend to walk beside him for a while. So we began walking along together.

Wild Thing shared about his dream to hike the Appalachian Trail. He was retired from the grocery business. As he told about his family, career, and dreams I quickly realized that "Wild Thing" was a trail name given by other hikers as a tease. It was like a lifelong friend of mine who was pretty large and went by the nickname of "Tiny."

We walked and talked over the next five miles before reaching a trail shelter. I shared that I was in no hurry to reach Hot Springs (the next trail town) and planned to camp here. Bill initially said that he was moving on to the next shelter, but then put down his pack and asked if I minded company. I told him he was welcome to stay. We visited, cooked supper together, and were joined just before dark by another hiker.

The next morning Bill started north before I did. After loading his pack on his shoulders, he came up and simply said, "Thanks for taking time to just walk with me and listen. I was lonely and ready to quit. I just needed a friend." I prayed with him and he gave me a big hug and started down the trail. I watched as his silhouette disappeared down the winding trail.

I never saw Bill again. I hiked all of that day and part of the next without seeing one single person. There is an eeriness in being silent and alone for that period of time. I more understood the loneliness that Bill was talking about after my two days of walking alone.

On the rest of that trip I was able to do plenty of writing. It was quiet and there was all of the solitude I needed. Writing and reflecting, I was glad I'd taken time to walk alongside a man who needed some encouragement.

I hope this book has been your companion as you've "walked along" these nearly two-hundred pages. If my stories have made your journey easier, my reason for writing and sharing them is satisfied.

Readers sometimes tell me, "I tried to slow down on reading each story, because I hated to reach the end of the book." My style of short stories is such that one can read at the pace desired. You can put it down for a day, week, or months, then pick it up again and meet an old friend.

I close with a fable from the Arabian Desert. The story is told of two travelers who stopped at an oasis while traveling through the desert. Before they reached this spot the sun had set. So in the dark, they pitched their tent beside the dry riverbed full of rocks.

During the darkest part of the night a voice spoke out,

"Pick up rocks and you will be both happy and sad."

The voice froze them with fear. Once again they heard,

"Pick up rocks and you will be both happy and sad."

Hurriedly they scampered to their feet and quickly loaded their camels in the pitch black darkness. Before leaving in fear they grabbed several small handfuls of rocks and pebbles and tossed them into their packs.

Being scared by the strange voice at the oasis, they rode non stop through the rest of the night. As dawn came, they finally felt safe enough to stop.

Discussing the strange voice with the cryptic message of "Pick up rocks and you'll be both happy and sad," they remembered the rocks they had scooped up in the darkness.

Opening their bags they were stunned to see that the rocks and pebbles they had gathered were really jewels and diamonds. And they were happy ...Yet they were also sad...

>They were happy... that they had gathered jewels...
>They were sad... that they had not gathered more.

As I finish my part of this book - the writing, I find myself both happy and sad... I'm happy to finish this book, (although I'm not sure you <u>ever</u> really finish a book!)

Yet, I'm also sad. To reach the end of a dream is great but sometimes is accompanied by a natural sadness. I've had to write, rewrite, and even cut some stories I loved and wanted to share with you. But there will be more stories, more books, and more sharing, God willing.

My final word to you is simply this:

Pick up stones which are really jewels... and gather as many as possible. The jewels I refer to are not material; they are instead friends, family, faith in God, joy through trials, and the happiness that comes to us through the gift of each new day.

Gather plenty of rocks, pick up those precious jewels, gather those priceless things around you... and you will find happiness... by listening to the wind in the pines all around you.

>Still gathering,

>Curt Iles

Curt Iles lives in Dry Creek, Louisiana with his wife, DeDe. They are the parents of three boys, Clay, Clint, and Terry. He is a graduate of both Louisiana College and McNeese State University.

He is the son of Clayton and Mary Iles. His family, including his two sisters, Colleen Glaser and Claudia Campbell, all still live in their hometown of Dry Creek.

Beginning in 1979, Iles worked as a science teacher, coach, and assistant principal, primarily at East Beauregard High School. For the past twelve years he has served as manager of Dry Creek Baptist Camp, a year round camp/retreat center for children, youth, and adults Visit www.drycreek.net to learn more about the camp's ministry.

Wind in the Pines is Iles' third book. His first two popular books of short stories are *Stories from the Creekbank* and *The Old House*. To learn more about these books, as well as new writing projects by Iles, visit www.creekbank.net.

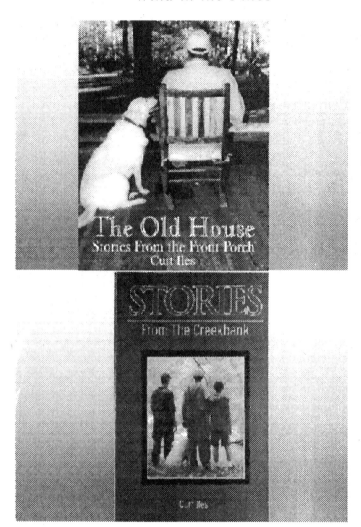

If you enjoyed "Wind in the Pines," you will also love Curt Iles' two earlier books. Available by contacting curtiles@aol.com, www.creekbank.net or by writing to: Curt Iles   P.O. Box 332 Dry Creek, LA 70637.